I0015217

ARDUINO

*Simple and Effective Strategies
to Arduino Programming*

Ethan Thorpe

Table of Contents

Introduction to Arduino

A rduino is an open-source platform which provides a low cost, simple interface to create microcontroller based projects. It's a great place to start learning and understanding the real-world application of embedded systems and how electronics work. its is extensively used for prototyping due to its low cost and easy connections to the microcontroller. The boards are versatile and have the peripherals for programming the microcontroller built-in, so no external programmers are required to program the microcontroller.

Arduino boards and Arduino IDE are open-source, meaning they are licenced in a way that anyone can use their designs and manufacture the boards which had led to competition and hence the low cost. It also ensures faster development of the boards and the IDE.

What is Arduino?

Arduino platform consists of various Arduino boards and the Arduino IDE (Integrated Development Environment), which consists of code editor to write the programs, a compiler to compile programs, and it is also used to program the Arduino boards.

Arduino ecosystem has grown many folds over the years and currently has many boards for all types of applications. Arduino boards are small microcontroller boards with other peripherals that have a number of connection sockets (GPIO), which can be used to connect different sensors and actuators to the board. The microcontroller is essentially the brain of the board, and it can be programmed to make any control system. The board also has a Universal Serial Bus plug (USB) to connect it to the computer. The board can be powered through this plug by computer or can be powered externally by a 9 volts battery. This port is also used to program the microcontroller on the board through the computer. The sensors and inputs, like the buttons, are essentially the things that help the microcontroller sense the environment; based on these inputs, the microcontroller take actions as per the program and changes its output.

Chapter 1

Basic Programming Concepts Needed To Get Started With Arduino

●─•+•───────●•+•●•+•●────────•+•●

In this chapter, we will introduce the basic programming concepts needed to get started with Arduino, as well as other types of similar embedded systems. To learn what you can build with these systems, see chapter 2. Since you want to learn about Arduino and embedded systems, explore all the chapters one after another of this book.

Here we will explain programming concepts from the start, and you don't need to know anything about Arduino or computer programming to get started. If you already have previous programming experience, this chapter may add some extra to your knowledge.

We will learn how a simple program works by making some modifications to it throughout the chapter. If you have access to an Arduino, you can use it throughout the chapter to practice the concepts learned, making the experience a lot nicer. You just need an Arduino, original or compatible, and nothing more. So go ahead.

This chapter is divided into the following parts:

- Overview
- Computer
- Computer program
- Programming language
- Algorithm (Program)
- Variable
  - Data Type
  - Assignment
- Operator
- Function
  - Function Call
  - Return Value
  - Parameters
- Comments
- Control Structures
  - While
  - For
  - If
  - If-else
- Libraries
- Conclusion

Overview

The purpose of this chapter is to quickly and easily present the basics of programming so you can start using Arduino in your projects without having to read many programming books or articles. The subject of "software development" as a whole is very broad, so let's focus only on the concepts that are important for Arduino and embedded systems in general.

There are many other things to learn about software that we won't cover here. In the next chapters, we have added information for you to follow to learn more advanced concepts or software concepts that are not widely used in embedded system programming.

Let's start by explaining how a computer works (remember that Arduino is, at the bottom, a computer).

Computer

A computer is simply a machine that processes instructions. These instructions are processed in the "brain" of the computer, which is called a microprocessor. Every computer has at least one microprocessor. Arduino, for example, is nothing but a very small computer, and it uses an ATmega microprocessor. Some microprocessors, such as ATmega, are also called microcontrollers.

Computer Program

A computer program, or software, is a sequence of instructions that are sent to the computer. Each type of microprocessor (brain) understands a different instruction set, i.e. its own "language." We also call this language machine language.

Machine languages are, at the bottom, the only languages that computers can understand, except that they are very difficult for humans to understand. That's why we use something called the programming language.

For systems like Arduino (so-called embedded systems), software that runs on the microprocessor is also called firmware.

Programming Language

We human beings need to convert our ideas into a form that computers can process, that is, machine language. Today's computers can't (yet) understand the natural language we use every day, so we need another special "language" to instruct the computer to do the tasks we want. This "language" is a programming language, and there are actually many of them.

These programming languages are also called high-level programming languages. The programming language used in Arduino is C ++ language (with minor modifications), which is a very traditional and well-known language. This is the language we will use throughout this book.

To convert a program written in a high-level machine language, we use something called a compiler. The action of turning a program to machine language is called compiling. To compile a program, usually using a development environment (or IDE, English Integrated Development Environment), which is a computer application with an integrated compiler, where you can write your program and compile it. In the case of Arduino, this development environment is the Arduino IDE.

Text containing the program in a high-level programming language is also known as the program source code.

Algorithm (Program)

An algorithm, or simply a program, is a way of telling a computer what it should do, in a way that we humans can easily understand. Algorithms are usually written in high-level programming languages. This applies to virtually any computer, including Arduino, where an algorithm is also known as sketching. For simplicity, from now on, we will refer to algorithms, programs, or sketches simply as "programs."

A program is made up of a sequence of commands, usually written in a text file. For this chapter, we will use the commands from the simpler Arduino program, Blink, which simply turns on and off an LED, and we will wreck it throughout the chapter. See below the source code of Blink:

```
int led = 13;
void  setup () {
pinMode (led, OUTPUT );
}
void  loop () {
    digitalWrite (led, HIGH );
    delay (1000);
    digitalWrite (led, LOW );
    delay (1000);
}
```

Variable

A variable is a feature used to store data in a computer program. Every computer has some kind of memory, and a variable represents a region of memory used to store certain information. This information can be, for example, a number, character, or text string. In order to use a variable in an Arduino program, we need to make a variable declaration, such as:

int led;

In this case, we are declaring a variable of the type installed led. Next, we will talk more about the data type of a variable.

Data Type

The data type of a variable means, as its name implies, the type of information that can be stored in that variable. In many programming languages, such as C ++, it is mandatory to define the data type at the time of variable declaration, as we saw in the variable declaration above. For Arduino modules that use ATmega processor, the most common types of data we use are:

- boolean: true (true) or false (false) value
- char: a character
- byte: one byte, or 8-bit string
- int: 16-bit signed integer (-32768 through 32767)
- unsigned int: 16-bit unsigned integer (0 to 65535)
- long: 16-bit signed integer (-2147483648 through 2147483647)
- unsigned long: 16-bit unsigned integer (0 to 4294967295)

- float: real precision single number (floating point)
- double: double precision real number (floating point)
- string: string
- void: empty type (no type)

For all data types supported by Arduino, see the "Data Types" section on this chapter.

Assignment

Assigning a value to a variable means storing the value in it for later use. The assignment command in C ++ is the =. To assign the value 13 to the variable led we created above, we do this:

```
led = 13;
```

When you store a value in a variable right at its initialization, we call it a variable initialization. So in our example program, we have:

```
int led = 13;
```

The purpose of this line of code is to say that Arduino pin 13 will be used to light the LED, and store this information for later use throughout the program.

Fixed values used in the program, such as the value 13above, are called constants because, unlike variables, their value does not change.

Operator

An operator is a set of one or more characters that serve to operate on one or more variables or constants. A very simple example of an operator is the addition operator, the +. Let's say we want to add two numbers and assign them to a variable x. For this, we do the following:

x = 2 + 3;

After executing the above command, the variable x will contain the value 5.

Each programming language has a different set of operators. Some of the most common operators in the C ++ language are:

- Arithmetic Operators:
  o +: addition ("more")
  o -: subtraction ("minus")
  o *: multiplication ("times")
  o /: division ("divided by")
- Logical Operators:
  o &&: conjunction ("e")
  o ||: disjunction ("or")
  o ==: equality ("equal to")
  o !=: inequality ("different from")
  o !: denial ("no")
  o >: "bigger then"
  o <: "less than"
  o >=: "greater than or equal to"
  o <=: "less than or equal to"

- Assignment Operators:
    o =: assigns a value to a variable, as we saw above.

As you develop your projects, you will gradually become familiar with all of these operators. For a complete list, see this Wikipedia page.

Function

A function is roughly a sequence of commands that can be reused multiple times throughout a program. To create a function and say what it does, we need to make a function declaration. See how a function is declared in our sample program:

```
void  setup () {
pinMode (led, OUTPUT );
}
```

Here we are declaring a function with the name setup(). What it does is execute the commands of another function pinMode(). The action of executing previously declared function commands is called a function call. We do not need to declare the function pinMode()because it is already declared automatically in the case of Arduino.

Function Call

Calling a function means executing the commands that were defined in your declaration. Once declared, a function can be called multiple times in the same program so that its commands can be executed again. To call our function setup(), for example, we would use the following command:

```
setup ();
```

However, in the case of Arduino, we do not need to call the function setup()because it is called automatically. When we compile a program in Arduino IDE, it calls the function setup()once and then calls the function loop()repeatedly until Arduino shuts down or restarts.

Return Value

The keyword that comes before the function name in the declaration defines the type of the function's return value. Every time a function is called, it is executed and returns or returns a certain value - this is the return value, or simply return of the function. The return value must have a type, which can be any of the data types mentioned above. In the case of our function setup(), the return type is void, which means that the function returns nothing.

For example, let's create a function that returns something, for example, an integer. To return a value, we use the command return:

```
int f () {
   return 1;
}
```

When called, the f()above function always returns the value 1. You can use the return value of a function to assign it to a variable. For example:

```
x = f ();
```

After declaring the function f()and calling the assignment command above, the variable x will contain the value 1.

Parameters

Another important feature of a function is the parameters. They serve to send some data to the function when it is called. Let's create, for example, a function that adds two numbers:

```
int soma ( int a, int b) {
   return a + b;
}
```

Here we just define a function called soma(), which accepts two integers as parameters. We need to name these parameters, in which case we choose a and b. These parameters act as variables that you can use within the function. Whenever we call the function sum(), we need to provide these two numbers. The command returns a + b; simply returns the function with the sum of the two numbers. Let's add 2 + 3 and assign the result to a variable x:

```
x = sum (2, 3);
```

After the above call, the variable x will contains the value 5.

Comments

A comment is a piece of text in your program that only serves to explain (document) the code without executing any kind of command in the program. Often, comments are also used to disable commands in code. In this case, we say that the code has been commented.

In the C ++ language, a comment can be written in two ways:

- Line comment: starts with the characters //, making all the rest of the current line a comment.

- Block Comment: Starts with characters /*and ends with characters */. All text between the beginning and the end becomes a comment and can consist of several lines.

For ease of viewing, development environments often show comments in a different color. For Arduino IDE, for example, comments are displayed in gray. Let's then explain what the sample program does by inserting several explanatory comments in it:

```
/ *
Programming for Arduino - Getting Started
Sample Program: Blink
* /

/ *
```

Led Variable Statement

Indicates that the LED is connected to Arduino digital pin 13 (D13).

```
* /
int led = 13;

/ *
```

Setup () Function Statement

This function is called only once when Arduino is started or restarted.

```
* /
void  setup () {
  // Call the pinMode () function that sets a pin as input or output
  pinMode (led, OUTPUT ); // Set the LED pin to output
}


/ *
```

Declaration of the loop ()

function After the setup () function is called, the loop () function is called repeatedly until

Arduino is turned off.

```
* /
void  loop () {
  // All following lines are called parameter passing
  function // Functions are executed in sequence to make the LED
light up and off
  digitalWrite (led, HIGH ); // Assigns high logic level to LED
pin, lighting it
  delay (1000);          // Wait 1000 milliseconds (one second)
  digitalWrite (led, LOW );  // Assign low logic level to LED pin,
deleting
  delay(1000);           // Wait 1000 milliseconds (one second)
```

// After finishing the loop () function, it is executed again and again,
    // so the LED keeps flashing.
    }

Control Structures

Control structures are blocks of instructions that alter the code execution flow of a program. With them, you can do things like execute different commands according to one condition or repeat a series of commands several times, for example.

The following are some of the most common control structures used in general programming languages. We will also modify our test program to exemplify better how these structures work.

While

The while loop is a structure that performs a set of commands over and over again as a certain condition is true. *While* in English means "while," and pronounced "wow-ou." It follows the following format:

```
while(condition) {
    ...
}
```

So let's make a modification to our program to better illustrate how while works. Our goal now is to make the LED flash three times, then wait five seconds, flash three more times, and so on. We will change the content of the function loop()to the following:

```
// Variable to count the number of times the LED flashed
int i = 0;

// Flash the LED three times
while (i <3) {
  digitalWrite (led, HIGH ); // Assigns high logic level to LED
pin, lighting it
  delay (1000);            // Wait 1000 milliseconds (one second)
  digitalWrite (led, LOW ); // Assigns low logic level to LED
pin, deleting it
  delay (1000);            // Wait 1000 milliseconds (one second)
  i = i + 1;               // Increase the number of times the LED
flashed
  }

delay (5000);             // Wait 5 seconds to flash the LED again
```

First, we declare a variable i. This variable will count how many times the LED has flashed since the beginning of the program or since the last pause of five seconds. We will initialize this variable to zero because at the beginning of the function loop(), the LED has not flashed once under these conditions.

Next, we enter the command while, which must be followed by a condition defined in parentheses. As long as this condition is true, the entire command block between characters {and } is executed repeatedly. In the case of our program, as long as the number of LED "flashes" (represented by the variable i) is less than three, we continue to execute the commands that make the LED flash. This is represented by the expression i < 3within the parentheses.

Between the characters {and }, we put the code that makes the LED blink, as before, but we must not forget to add 1to the variable that counts the number of "blinks." This is done in the following line of code:

```
    i = i + 1;            // Increase the number of times the LED
  flashed
```

Note that after executing all commands between {and }, we will always have in the variable i the number of times the LED has flashed since the start of the function loop(). Let's go through the sequence of steps executed each time the function loop()is called:

1. We assigned 0the variable i: the LED has not flashed once.

2. We compare if i < 3: as 0is smaller than 3, we execute the commands between {and }:

   I.   We execute the commands to turn the LED on and off.

   II. We add 1to the variable i, making it 1: we know that the LED flashed once.

3. We go back to the beginning of while and compare if i < 3: as it 1is smaller than 3, we execute the commands between {and }again:

   I.   We execute the commands to turn the LED on and off.

II.   We added 1the variable i, making it 2: we know that the LED flashed twice.

4. We go back to the beginning of while and compare if i < 3: as it 2is smaller than 3, we execute the commands between {and }again:

  I.   We execute the commands to turn the LED on and off.

  II.   We added the 1 variable to i to make it 3: we know that the LED flashed three times.

1. We go back to the beginning of the while and compare if i < 3: since 3 it is no smaller than 3, we no longer execute the commands between {and }and proceed to the next statement.

2. We waited five seconds through the call delay(5000).

After these steps, we reach the end of the function loop(), and as we already know, it is called again by the Arduino system. This restarts the cycle by performing the above steps indefinitely.

Run the modified program with the instructions above on your Arduino and try to vary the number of "blinks" and the number

For

Now that we have learned the while command, it is very easy to learn the for command, as it is almost the same thing. Let's modify the content of the function loop()as we did above, but using the for instead of while:

```
// Variable to count the number of times the LED flashed
int i;

// Flash LED three times
for (i = 0; i <3; i ++) {
    digitalWrite (led, HIGH ); // Assigns high logic level to LED
pin, lighting it
    delay (1000);          // Wait 1000 milliseconds (one second)
    digitalWrite (led, LOW );  // Assigns low logic level to LED
pin, deleting it
    delay (1000);          // Wait 1000 milliseconds (one second)
}

delay (5000);          // Wait 5 seconds to flash the LED again
```

The first modification we made was to declare the variable i without initializing it with the value 0. We can do that because the command will do it for us. It follows the following format:

```
for(boot; condition; finishing) {
    ...
}
```

Let's describe each item separately:

- **Condition:** is a repeatedly verified expression, identical to the condition in parentheses of a while. As long as it is true, commands enter {and }continue to execute.

- **Initialization:** This is a command executed only once at the beginning of the command for.

- **Termination:** is a command executed repeatedly at the end of each command execution between {and }.

We can then verify that for nothing is more than a while plus a boot command, and a terminate command. For our test program, these commands are respectively:

- i = 0: Initializes the count of the number of "blinks."

- i++: sum 1to the variable i at the end of command execution between {and }; in this case it is equivalent to the command i = i + 1. The operator ++is called the increment operator, and is widely used in the C ++ language.

If we run the above program on Arduino, we will see that the result is the same as we got with the program we did earlier using a while.

If

The if is one of the basic structures in general programming. If stands for "if" in English, and that is exactly what it does: it checks an expression and, only if it is true, executes a set of commands. In natural language, he executes a logic like, " If this is true, then do that."

To illustrate, let's modify our sample program so that it does the same thing we did with while and for above, but let's do it using one if, which follows the following format:

```
if(condition) {
    ...
}
```

The logic is very simple: whenever the condition is true, the commands enter {and } are executed, otherwise the program proceeds without executing them. Let's see how the function looks like loop():

```
// Variable to count the number of times the LED flashed
int i = 0;

void  loop () {
   digitalWrite (led, HIGH ); // Assigns high logic level to LED
pin, lighting it
   delay (1000);          // Wait 1000 milliseconds (one second)
   digitalWrite (led, LOW );  // Assigns low logic level to LED pin,
deleting it
   delay (1000);          // Wait 1000 milliseconds (one second)

   i ++;                  // Increment the number of "blinks"
   if (i == 3) {
      delay (5000);       // Wait 5 seconds to flash the LED again
      i = 0;              // Reset the number of "blinks" counter
   }
}
```

Here the logic is a bit different: we will keep the function loop()flashing the LED as in the original program, but we will insert an additional 5 seconds wait after every 3 flashes. For this, we create a variable **i** outside the function loop(); it must be declared from outside the function in order to retain its value between each execution of the function loop(). We call this the **global variable**. When the variable is declared within the function body, it does not retain the value between each execution and is restarted each time the function is re-executed. We call this the **local variable**.

We will then use this global variable **i** to count, again, the number of times the LED went on and off. In the variable declaration, we initialize it with the value 0to indicate that the LED has not lit up yet. The function loop()then starts executing by turning the LED on and off. To count the number of times the LED flashed, we added the following line of code:

    i ++;   // Increase number of "blinks"

We then use the if to check if we have just lit the LED for the third time. For this, we use the expression i == 3in the condition of if. If this expression is true, that is to say, that the LED has already lit 3 times, then we insert an additional 5 second pause with the call delay(5000) and restart the number of "blinks" again with the following command:

    i = 0;   // Reset the number of "blinks" counter

From then on, the function loop()continues to be called, and the cycle starts again.

If-else

The if-else, also known as if-then-else it can be seen as an extension command if. Else in English means "otherwise,"and he does exactly what the name says:" If that's true, then do that, otherwise do something else." It follows the following format:

```
if(condition) {
   ...
} else {
   ...
}
```

To illustrate, let's use the program is that we show up, but this time we will make the LED on and off four times before giving a five-second pause. Then we will make the third of each of these four "flashes" light up for a shorter period. Within the function loop(), we will have the following:

```
// Variable to count the number of times the LED flashed
int i;

// Flash the LED three times
for (i = 0; i <3; i ++) {
   if (i == 2) {
      digitalWrite (led, HIGH ); // Assigns high logic level to LED
pin, lighting it
      delay (200);          // Wait 200 milliseconds (one second)
      digitalWrite (led, LOW );  // Assigns low logic level to LED
pin, deleting it
      delay (1800);          // Wait 1800 milliseconds (one second)
   } else {
      digitalWrite (led, HIGH ); // Assign high logic level to LED
pin, lighting it
```

```
    delay (1000);           // Wait 1000 milliseconds (one second)
    digitalWrite (led, LOW );  // Assigns low logic level to LED
pin, deleting it
    delay (1000);           // Wait 1000 milliseconds (one second)
  }
}


    delay (5000);           // Wait 5 seconds to flash the LED again
```

Here what we do is, every time we turn on the LED, check if this is the third time this happens, by command if with the condition **i** == **2**. If this expression is true, it means that we have already lit the LED twice and are about to light it for the third time; In this case we change the time that the LED is random to a smaller value of 0.2 seconds (a reduction of 0.8 seconds) and the time it turns off to a larger value of 1.8 seconds (increase of 0 seconds). , 8 seconds).

But what if this is not the third time the LED has been on? This is where o else: If the condition of if is true, the command block between {and }after if is executed, otherwise the block between {and }after else is executed. This means that for the first, second, and fourth "blinks," the default time of one second will be used.

Libraries

The things we learned in the previous sections are important for implementing the logic of your Arduino program, but you will usually want to do more than just light a LED. When you do more complex tasks or use some other circuit connected to your Arduino, a very important feature is libraries.

A library is basically made up of additional source code that you add to your project through the include command. Let's see how to add, for example, a library for controlling a liquid crystal display (LCD):

#include < LiquidCrystal .h>

An Arduino library usually presents itself as one or more classes that have functions, methods, to trigger devices, configure them, or perform some other task. Continuing with the example of the LCD display, to use it in your program, you must first initialize it. What we do in this case is create an object to access the LCD (technically, this is called instantiating an object). Let's see how this is done:

LiquidCrystal LCD (12, 11, 5, 4, 3, 2);

When we do this, lcd it becomes an object of the class LiquidCrystal. This is the equivalent of creating a variable of type LiquidCrystal. The parameters that are passed in parentheses serve to initialize the configuration of this object, in which case they correspond to the pin numbers that were used to connect the LCD to the Arduino.

Arduino libraries almost always have a method begin(), which serves to make the initial configuration of the device being controlled. To call the function begin()of the object lcd we created, we do the following:

lCD begin (16, 2);

This method begin()is usually called from within the function setup(), i.e. during program startup. The method parameters in begin()this case correspond to the number of columns and the number of rows of the LCD, respectively.

After these steps, we can now write a text on the LCD. We do this using the print()object method lcdwhenever we need it throughout the program:

    lcd print ("Hi!");

The method print()is just one of several methods available in the library LiquidCrystal. To know all the methods provided by a particular library, you need to refer to the documentation provided with it.

This is the basic process of using libraries in Arduino. For more information, read the documentation provided with the library you are using.

Classes, objects, and methods are object-oriented programming concepts. We won't explain everything in detail here, but if you want to learn more about it, follow the related links at the bottom of the page.

Conclusion

In this chapter we look at the basic programming concepts required to program an Arduino or even other embedded hardware platforms. But this is only the beginning, and there is still much to learn, both in hardware and software. Through the next chapter of this book, there are interesting sections and lessons so you can learn more advanced concepts and expand your possibilities.

Chapter 2

Getting Started with Arduino

If you work with electronics, you probably know or have heard about Arduino before you start reading this book. If you are from some other area, say art and design, you have probably heard about this open-source development platform as well. The Arduino is a project that has become popular throughout the world because of its practicality, ease of work and competitive price.

In this chapter, we'll introduce what your hardware and software aspects are, how they came about, as well as a step-by-step lesson to set up an initial desktop and implement your first project with Arduino.

By the end of this chapter, you are expected to be able to explain and understand what the Arduino system consists of and also be able to start developing your first applications. Move on!

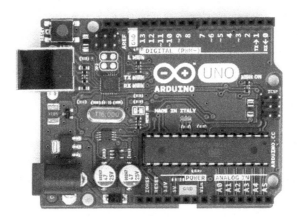

Arduino UNO Rev 3 Platform.

What Is Arduino and Why Use It?

In a nutshell, Arduino is an electronic project development platform (or electronic prototyping, as it is also commonly said), consisting of both hardware and software, and which is available under the Creative Commons Attribution-Share-Alike license.

This means that all Arduino project design files are freely available on the internet and that their software is open source. Also, the platform may be used for both personal and business purposes, provided that credits are attributed to the Arduino brand, and project files are also made available under the same license.

The project emerged in Italy in 2015 from a group of developers led by Massimo Banzi. The initial purpose was to create a low-cost, easy-to-work platform that could be used by students to develop their prototypes efficiently and cheaply. It was also thought to assist in the teaching of electronics to art and design students, particularly to create interactive environments, something very much in vogue within contemporary design and arts.

The main reasons for using the Arduino platform in your projects are as follows:

- Low-cost prototyping

- Free simulation software available

- Easy to program

- A large number of tutorials, articles, and projects ready on the internet

- Extensive community of developers and hobbyists

- No experience or extensive prior knowledge of electronics/programming required (however, it is advisable to know the basics at least)

Arduino is not the only electronic prototyping platform on the market. There are other projects and development kits, the most common being Raspberry Pi and BeagleBone. Each uses a different microcontroller and has hardware design with its own characteristics. Prices also vary widely, and some other platforms are not as popular.

The choice of which prototyping kit to use depends on the demands and needs your project imposes. Certainly, given the reasons cited above, Arduino is a strong candidate for most of its projects.

An Overview of Arduino

Arduino is a prototyping platform that enables the development of various robotic projects, acting as a type of simplified programmable electronic brain, with several ports for connections to modules and sensors.

It is designed using a specific programming microcontroller with analog and digital input and output pins, as well as pins for power and I2C protocol, for example.

Arduino was so successful after its inception that within a few years, it became known in schools and universities around the world, becoming a low-cost, extremely functional global fever.

It is noteworthy that since its inception was implemented as open-source, i.e., has a free hardware concept, which in practice means that it can be modified and improved in various ways.

In short, Arduino is an open-source electronics prototyping platform and free hardware very easy to use and use. It has been designed through a specific programming microcontroller with power and signal input and output pins that can be easily applied to the most diverse electronic and electrical projects.

Who Invented Arduino?

Arduino was invented by Massimo Banzi, the co-founder of the prototyping platform, together with 4 other researchers: David Cuartielles, Gianluca Martino, David Mellis, and Tom Igoe in 2005.

At this time, professor of electronics and programming Massimo wanted to teach his students of the design course basics of electronics and programming in order to stimulate the development of robotics, interactivity and art projects, but soon came across a problem, not There were affordable plates, let alone simplified layouts for students who were just entering this area.

From the beginning of the project development, the founders' main objective was to create a cheap electronic device with great functionality, and at the same time, that could be easily programmed.

This explains the great success that the Arduino has achieved, appearing in low, medium, and high complexity robotic designs, allowing the integration with electronic modules and sensors of the most diverse types.

Some scholars in the area say that the microcontroller was named after Arduino after King Arduin, who ruled northern Italy in the year 1002 and was a striking figure. Massimo still had a bar in the town of Ivre called Bar di Re Arduino, already inspired by the king.

How does Arduino Work?

Arduino works from programming codes, where it can be freely used for various types of functions and can control everything from electronic sensors to highly complex modules.

The programming is done through the IDE program Arduino, which can be downloaded directly from the official website arduino.cc, in addition, the connection to the computer is made via USB cable, allowing the commands defined in the program to be correctly transferred to board.

After recording the codes according to the chosen sensors, it can be installed at random locations using power supplies or even batteries if it needs to be in an isolated location.

It is important to mention that the sensors can be connected directly to their communication ports using jumpers or on test plates, known as protoboards.

Both hardware and software are designed to assist designers, hobbyists, hackers, artists, novices, and anyone interested in creating interactive equipment and environments. Arduino can interact with sensors, motors, cameras, shields, and most known electronics.

The Arduino Uno is the best-known model, with 13 digital ports, 6 analog ports, 3 GND ports, a 5V port, and a 3.3V port, as well as other configuration and power pins.

Among the Arduino digital pins, it is worth remembering that there are some pins that differ from the others because they have their own characteristics such as PWM pins that have a "~" before the number and have the ability to vary the output signal to control motors, for example, pins 0 (RX) and 1 (TX) which are communication pins.

As for power, it can be done through the USB port, with the possibility of the programmer choosing to use an external source with a direct connection to the Arduino p4 jack.

How to Program an Arduino

Arduino programming is done via software on the computer or directly on an android phone; in any case, the program needs to be downloaded from the manufacturer's website and installed directly on the machine.

After that, you need to connect the card with the USB cable, which is usually included, and select the desired card, and then you have to upload a ready-made code or create one from scratch in C language.

C programming is a universal language that is taught in technical and higher information technology courses. In any case, as it is a simple method, it can easily be learned from a reading of books and articles available on the Internet.

Programming has ceased to be considered a "seven-headed animal" and has become a means of teaching, a means of challenging our own limits, and especially a fun experience that increasingly infects adults and children regardless of their age, from the simplest — projects even the most complex programming schemes.

How much does an Arduino Cost?

The Arduino costs between $ 350 and R $ 5,000 on average, it does not have an exactly defined value, because it is a type of microcontroller that is divided into many models, from the smallest and easiest models to use to the complete models with several extra functions.

The best known models are:

- Arduino Uno R3
- Arduino Mega2560
- Arduino Nano
- Arduino Micro
- and Arduino DUE.

It has many variations because it is an open-source project, which may lower or increase the prices mentioned above.

This is not to say that you will need an expensive microcontroller to have the special functions because, with a simple one like UNO, you will be able to install any extra modules that can even pass the functionality of the complete model, everything will depend on the type of project that you want to develop.

What to do with Arduino

With Arduino, many electronic projects can be created, including robotic trolleys and arms, battle robots, line-following robots, home automation projects, and more.

For those just starting out and still wondering what the best Arduino to start with, keep in mind that the Arduino UNO is currently the "standard" card on the market and probably the best choice for those starting with this line of controllers.

Have you ever come across a rising light with your simple presence, clapping, or varying ambient light? Maybe you have seen carts that follow a line, dodging obstacles, receiving commands through mobile phones, these are two of the main electronic movements involving Arduino, Home Automation and Robotics.

Through Arduino UNO, it is possible to develop a wide range of interactive objects and autonomous environments by simply assembling your project physically, connecting Arduino with your computer, and through a specific platform available for download at the link below to perform the recording process.

Where to start?
After learning a little more about this amazing card in this "An overview of Arduino?" section, Just pick a model and start studying the next content of this book, surely you will be amazed at how many things can be automated in your home and improved — their projects, whether at science fairs or robotics competitions.

The Hardware of Arduino
Let's talk a little about what Arduino hardware. All information present here is available on the official Arduino website and move further with this book to explore it.

There is not just one Arduino model. There are several cards available, each with different levels of complexity and different functionality. There are 6 classes of Arduino prototyping platforms available on the market today. Are they:

- **Entry Level:** Simpler versions focused on who is starting to develop electronic projects.

- **Enhanced Features:** Cards with additional functionality for more complex designs.

- **Internet of Things:** Specific platforms for IoT projects.

- **Education:** Just a model of this class, focused on the teaching of electronics and programming.

- **Wearable:** Platforms with specific features for the development of wearables, or "wearable technologies" such as smartwatches and embedded electronics garments.

- **3D printing:** 3D printer developed with Arduino.

Let's focus on Arduino UNO, an entry-level card, and one of the most popular and most affordable models. It is an ideal card for those who are taking their first steps in electronics and the Arduino universe.

As seen in figure 1, the board has a number of available connector pins and connectors for interfacing with the outside world. The MCU is an ATmega328p (datasheet). The main features of the board are:

- 14 digital I / Os, of which 6 can be used as PWM

- 6 Analog Inputs

- 16MHz Oscillator

- USB connector

- Power connector

- ICSP header

- Reset button

The card can be powered by both USB cable and AC / DC adapter. All features of the microcontroller are available to interface with the outside world. In general, analog inputs are used to read external sensors, and PWM outputs and digital outputs are used to control motors and actuators and drive drivers for external loads.

The Software of Arduino

The Arduino IDE is also open source. Its graphical environment was developed in Java and based on Processing and other open-source languages. The programming environment is available for Windows, MAC and Linux. The download can be done directly on the official page.

The programming language used to write Arduino code is based on traditional C / C ++ (with modifications) and has a very high degree of abstraction and a number of libraries that encapsulate most of the microcontroller complexity.

This high degree of abstraction and library set are largely responsible for making programming more intuitive and fast, as the developer does not need to know the registers, memory details, and dynamics processor.

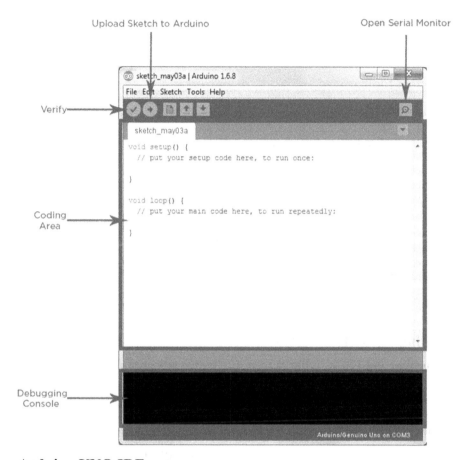

Arduino UNO IDE.

We see that IDE is very simple and lean.

At the top, we have the following tabs: File, Edit, Sketch, Tools and Help. This last one is interesting always to be frequented by the user because it has important references and is the main source of information and troubleshooting.

Just below this main menu are some shortcut icons. They are (from left to right):

Shortcut toolbar.

- Verify: Identify syntax errors in code
- Upload: Loads software on board
- New: Creates a New Blank Sketch Tab
- Open: Opened a Sketchbook Sketch
- Save: Save Sketch in Development

In the next couple of chapter, you will learn more about Arduino programming and C / C ++ languages.

Getting Ready to Program Arduino
Now that we know what Arduino's hardware and software features are let's prepare and configure our development setup.

From a hardware standpoint, simply power the card and connect the USB cable to the computer. The IDE does all other settings. See the steps below:

- Power and connect Arduino to PC via USB cable

- In the IDE, select the board model

  o Open Tools tab, select Board option and then select Arduino Uno

- Select serial port to which the card has been assigned

  o Open the Tools tab, select the Serial Port option and then select the COMX port, where X is the number the PC has associated with the serial port assigned to Arduino.

After these settings, the IDE is ready to load programs developed in Arduino and run any available example.

Programming the First Application

Let's now make the first example in Arduino. The simplest example, usually the first made to test a board or when learning for the first time, is the famous "Led Blink," that is, let's write a program to make a led flash.

The Arduino UNO platform has an onboard led previously connected to the logic state of pin 13. So we can use this led to our example.

Another good news is that IDE has a good and complete library of examples that can be used as a basis for a wide range of applications. To access the Led Blink example, go to Files → Examples → Basics → Blink.

In the following figure, we see the code of this example:

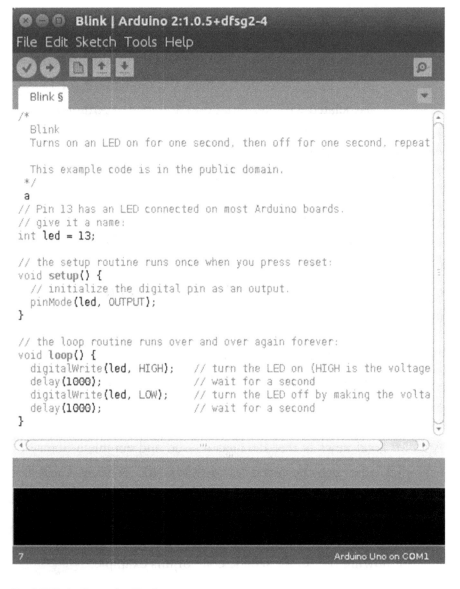

```
/*
  Blink
  Turns on an LED on for one second, then off for one second, repeat

  This example code is in the public domain.
*/
a
// Pin 13 has an LED connected on most Arduino boards.
// give it a name:
int led = 13;

// the setup routine runs once when you press reset:
void setup() {
  // initialize the digital pin as an output.
  pinMode(led, OUTPUT);
}

// the loop routine runs over and over again forever:
void loop() {
  digitalWrite(led, HIGH);    // turn the LED on (HIGH is the voltage
  delay(1000);                // wait for a second
  digitalWrite(led, LOW);     // turn the LED off by making the volta
  delay(1000);                // wait for a second
}
```

Led Blink Sample Code.

In the example above, we can see the two parts that will always be present in all your Arduino projects. The void Setup() function and the void loop () function. The first is responsible for configuring and

42

making all the necessary settings for a given application. For example, in the case of Led Blink, we see the line: pinMode (Led, OUTPUT).

This line of code is responsible for initializing the digital ports as outputs. Other settings, such as PWM signal frequency, port initialization as input, serial channel settings, among others, are all made in this function.

The second routine consists of the infinite loop that will be repeated throughout the application. That is, after Arduino is energized, the first piece of software that will run is the void setup () function, and soon after, the software enters the void loop () routine, and repeats the code within that routine continuously. It is in this infinite loop that the code for the application itself must be placed.

In the case of Led Blink, we have the following code in the infinite loop:

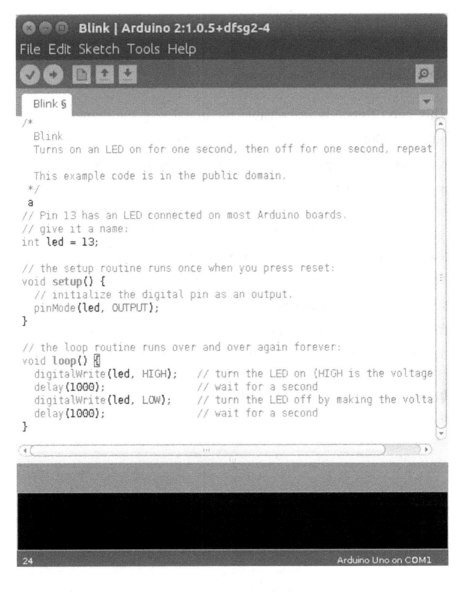

```
/*
  Blink
  Turns on an LED on for one second, then off for one second, repeat

  This example code is in the public domain.
*/
a
// Pin 13 has an LED connected on most Arduino boards.
// give it a name:
int led = 13;

// the setup routine runs once when you press reset:
void setup() {
  // initialize the digital pin as an output.
  pinMode(led, OUTPUT);
}

// the loop routine runs over and over again forever:
void loop() {
  digitalWrite(led, HIGH);    // turn the LED on (HIGH is the voltage
  delay(1000);                // wait for a second
  digitalWrite(led, LOW);     // turn the LED off by making the volta
  delay(1000);                // wait for a second
}
```

Led Blink application code present in infinite loop.

This code calls the digitalWrite (led, High) function, which assigns a high level to the led pin, which in this case corresponds to pin 13 (note in figure 6 that led is an integer variable to which the value 13 has been assigned) , i.e. the led connected to pin 13 is activated.

44

Next is called the delay (1000) function, which pauses the loop for a thousand milliseconds, that is, for one second.

After waiting for this time, the digitalWrite () function is called again, but this time to assign a low logic level to pin 13, i.e. to turn off the led connected to pin 13. Finally, the delay function (1000) is again call to pause another second.

This way, the led flashes at continuous intervals of one second. Here's our example Led Blink! Simple, isn't it ?!

To upload the code on the board, just click the Upload icon. The firmware will be written to the board's Atmel microcontroller, and the first flashing application will be ready. Each time the Arduino is energized, the pin 13 led will flash at regular one-second intervals.

Fritzing Arduino Application Simulation
It is a common and highly recommended practice that every electronics project be first simulated via software before it is mounted on hardware. In addition to being a good practice that allows developers to debug and identify firmware errors even before boarding the platform, simulators also allow applications to be developed without the board necessarily being present.

A very popular simulator for Arduino circuits is Fritzing. It is open-source software that has an excellent and intuitive graphical interface.

If you have come this far, then you already know what the Arduino platform is and how it works. The Led Blink example is a very basic application, and we recommend that you explore the other examples available in the IDE and follow the blog posts here. There is a great documentary that we highly recommend about Arduino history and how it all started (see here!).

The Arduino platform allows anyone to develop microcontroller electronic applications, and was a milestone in the popularization of interactive systems in the design and arts fields, as it made the lives of many non-electronics professionals much easier.

For those who work in electronics, whether as a professional or as a hobby, Arduino allows you to prototype and implement projects quickly and inexpensively, so you don't have to go through giant datasheets or crush handcrafted boards looking for problems. Hands-on!

New Arduino IDE - Professional - PRO IDE
For those who do not believe it is possible to do Professional Projects with Arduino, this is an IDE (Development Platform) designed just for that. Very interesting! But it is still in the development phase so that it may present errors.

The simplicity of the Arduino IDE has made it one of the most popular in the world - it's easy enough for beginners and fast for advanced users. Millions of people have used it as their daily tool for programming projects and applications. However, we have listened to your comments, and the time has come for a new, enhanced version with features that will appeal to the most advanced developers among you - continuing with the simple, classic Arduino IDE that many of you are familiar with.

Key features of this initial alpha release of the new Arduino Pro IDE are:

- Modern and complete development environment
- Dual Mode, Classic Mode (identical to Arduino's classic IDE) and Pro Mode (File System view)
- Ninth Board Manager
- New Library Manager
- Board List
- Basic Autofill
- Git integration
- Serial monitor
- Dark mode

But the new architecture opens the door to the features requested by the Arduino community that will follow shortly:

- Sketch Sync with Arduino Create Editor
- Debugger
- Fully open to third party plugins
- Support for additional non-C ++ languages

The new Arduino Pro IDE is based on the latest technologies:

- The Arduino CLI running in daemon mode provides all major Arduino features.

- The application frontend is based on the open-source Eclipse Theia IDE.

- Electron, the framework behind Eclipse Theia, enables the use of web technologies in desktop environments.

Available on Windows, Mac OS X, and Linux64 versions.

For those who love and appreciate Arduino's classic IDE, don't worry, it will remain available forever.

Chapter 3

C Language Basics

General Considerations

Many languages have been developed and for many years used for different purposes and characteristics, such as Fortran, Cobol, Basic, Algol, Pascal, and so on. But what is C? C is the name of a language currently used in different areas and purposes. It is now part of an advanced language developed at Bell Labs in the 1970s.

The formal definition of language can be found in the book "The C Programming Language" by Brian W. Kernighan and Dennis M. Ritchie (the parents of language). In the 1980s, work began on creating a standard called C ANSI (American National Standardization Institute).

It is a medium level language, as it can work at a level close to the machine level or as a high-level language like existing ones.

With C, we can write concise, organized, and easy-to-understand programs, but unfortunately, lack of discipline can lead to poorly written programs that are difficult to read and understand. It should not be forgotten that C is a language for programmers as it imposes few restrictions on what can be done. C is friendly and structured to encourage good programming habits; it is up to the programmer to exercise these habits.

The need to write programs that make use of machine language resources in a simpler and more portable way meant that the main use of C was the rewriting of UNIX operating systems. Its indication is mainly in the development of programs such as compilers, interpreters, text editors, databases. Computer graphics, image manipulation, and processing, process control…

Key features of C language to consider:

- Portability
- Generation of fast and compact executable codes
- Interaction with the operating system
- Ease of use (through environments such as Borland C ++ 5.0)
- Structured Language
- Reliability
- Simplicity

Basic Elements

Identifiers

They are used to name constants, variables, functions, and various user-defined objects. The rules for forming these names are:

1. Every identifier must start with a letter (a..z or A..Z) or underscore

2. May not contain special symbols. After the first character can be used: letters, underscores and / or digits.

3. Identifiers of a maximum of 32 characters are used as they are significant.

4. It cannot be a reserved word or name of library functions.

Note: Upper and lower case letters are treated differently.

Basic Data Types

Type	Number of bytes	Scale
char	1	-128 to 127
Int	2	-32768 to 32767
float	4	3.4E-38 to 3.4E + 38 (+ -)
double	8th	1.7E-308 to 1.7E + 308 (+ -)
void	0	worthless

Modifiers

Type	Number of bytes	Scale
Unsigned char	1	0 to 255
unsigned int	2	0 to 65535
Short int	2	-32768 to 32767
unsigned short int	2	0 to 65535
long int	4	-2147483648 to 2147483647
unsigned long int	4	0 to 4294967295
long double	10	3.4E-4932 to 1.1E + 4932

Comments:

1. The signed modifier may eventually be used, but its use is equivalent to using a type without any modifier.

2. The word int can be omitted. Ex: unsigned long int □ unsigned long

Declaration of Variables

The general form for declaring a variable is:

variable_type   variable_list;

where variable_type is a valid type in C (Sections 1.2 and 1.3), and variable_list can be one or more comma-separated identifier names.

Examples:

> int f, i, k; / * all variables of type int * /
> float a, A, b; / * all float variables * /

Constants

In C, constants are fixed values that cannot be changed by a program.

Constants in Decimal Basis

1. Integer numerical constants: can be assigned to char and int variables, modified or not, depending on the value of the constant and the range of values accepted by the variable.

   Examples: 345   10   0   5000000

2. Noninteger numerical constants: can be assigned to float and double variables, modified or not, depending on the value of the constant and the range of values accepted by the variable.

   Examples: -56,897 1.2E + 5

3.   Character constants: can be assigned to char- type variables, modified or not. The value of the constant is equal

to the numeric value of the ASCII table of the character represented by " (commonly referred to as "single")

Constants in Hexadecimal and Octal Bases

Hexadecimal constants start with 0x, while octal constants start with 0.

Examples: 0xAB (hexadecimal)   016 (octal)

String Constants (Strings)

They are represented in quotation marks.

Example: "This is a string constant."

C Language Control Characters

These characters must be represented as alphanumeric characters (in ") or as the content of a string.

Code	Meaning
\The	audible signal
\B	cursor backspace
\ f	form feed

\n	new line
\r	car return
\t	horizontal tab
\'	quotation marks
\'	apostrophe
\0	null (zero)
\\	backslash
\v	vertical tab
\The	beep
\N	octal constant (where N is octal)
\xN	hexadecimal constant (where N is hexadecimal)

Instructions

A C language statement is an expression followed by a semicolon. It can be an assignment, a function call, a deviation test, or a loop test.

Example assignment statement: x = 12;

Where the equal sign (=) is the assignment operator. Note that the left operand of the assignment operator is always a variable and that the right operand must be of a data type compatible with the type of the variable.

Operators

Arithmetic Operators

Addition	+
Subtraction	-
Division	/
Multiplication	*
Rest	%

Comments:

1. All operators are defined for integer and noninteger types except the remainder (%) operator, which is not defined for variables of noninteger types.

2. For any integer type, adding one to the largest track number of that type produces the smallest track number. Overflow errors are not always detected, so the programmer must be

careful when sizing program variables so that they do not occur.

Example:

unsigned char x;

x = 255;

x = x + 1; / * x should assume 256, however it overflows the range and returns to the smallest value that is 0 * /

Relational Operators

Less than	<
Bigger then	>
Less or equal	<=
Bigger or equal	> =
Equality	= =
Inequality	! =

Comments:

1. All relational operations result in an integer representing a logical value (1 = true and 0 = false).

2. Do not confuse the assignment operator (=) with the equality operator (= =).

Logical Operators

and (conjunction)	&&
or (disjunction)	||
no (denial)	!

Logical operators can receive any operand value, but nonzero values are always interpreted as true, and zero values are interpreted as false. The result of a logical operation is always a logical value.

Truth table:

P	Q	p && q	p || what	!P
0	0	0	0	1
0	1	0	1	1
1	0	0	1	0
1	1	1	1	0

Combined Assignment Operators

$+=$ $-=$ $*=$ $/=$

Examples:

a += b; / * a = a + b; * /

a -= b; / * a = a - b; * /

a * = b; / * a = a * b; * /

a / = b; / * a = a / b; * /

Comments:

1. All assignment operators assign the result of an expression to a variable. If the left side type is not the same as the right side type, the right side type will be converted to the left side type. This can cause loss of accuracy in some data types and should be taken seriously by the programmer.

Postfix and Prefixed Operators

Operator	Meaning
++ variable	increment the variable before using its value
Variable ++	increment the variable after using its value
- variable	decrement the variable before using its value
Variable -	decrement the variable after using its value

Examples:

int a, b, c;

a = 6;

b = ++ a; / * a gets 7 then b also gets 7 * /

c = a ++; / * c gets 7 and then gets 8 * /

Bit Level Operators

Shift left	<<
Shift right	>>
and (and)	&
or (or)	|
or exclusive (xor)	^
not not)	~

For further discussion on the use of bits and binary numbers, see the text on Numerical Bases.

Address Operators

& - return variable address

* - return the contents of the address stored in a pointer variable

To learn more about address operators, see Pointers.

Other Operators

sizeof (operand) - provides the size in bytes of your operand

Ex:

    int x;

    float y;

    char c;

    x = sizeof (int); / * gives the size of type int (2 bytes) * /

    x = sizeof (y); / * gives the size of variable y (4 bytes) * /

    x = sizeof (c);   / * gives the size of variable c (1 byte) * /

Expressions

Operators, constants, variables, and functions are expressions. The main algebraic rules are considered in the expressions. Some aspects of expressions are C language-specific and are explained below.

Automatic Type Conversion

When constants, variables, and functions of different types are mixed into one expression, they are all converted to the largest operand type. This is done operation by operation according to the following rules:

1. All operands of type char and short int are converted to int. All float operands are converted to double.

2. For all pairs of operands involved in an operation, if one of them is long double the other operand is converted to a long double. If one is double, the other is converted to double. If one is long, the other is converted to long. If one is unsigned, the other is converted to unsigned.

Example:

    float x, res;

    char c;

    ...

res = x / c; / * the value of x / c is converted to a float, although c is originally a char * /

Explicit Type Casts

You can force an expression to be of a specific type without, however, changing the types of variables involved in this expression. This type of operation is called explicit type cast, or type cast.

The general form of a type cast is:

(type) expression;

where type is one of the default C language data types.

Type cast operations are very useful in expressions where some operation results in loss of precision due to the type of variables or constants involved. For example:

float res;

int op1, op2;

op1 = 3;

op2 = 2;

res = op1 / op2; / * res gets 1 since op1 and op2 are both

int numbers and the result of their

division is also int * /

res = (float) op1 / op2; / * res gets 1.5 as type cast

forced the op1 operand to be a float

In this operation. The result of the division,

therefore it is also float * /

Spacing and Parentheses

We can put spaces in an expression to make it more readable. Using redundant or additional parentheses will not cause errors or slow the expression's execution speed.

Example:

a = b / 9.67-56.89 * x-34.7;

a = (b / 9.67) - (56.89 * x) - 34.7; / * equivalent * /

Structure of a C program

An interesting feature of program C is its modular and functional aspect, where the main program itself is a function. This form of language presentation facilitates the development of programs, as it allows the use of structured and modular forms found in other languages.

The structure of a C program has the following elements, and those enclosed in brackets are optional:

```
[        preprocessing settings        ]
[          type definitions                    ]
[          global variable declarations    ]
[          function prototypes                ]
[          functions                                   ]

main ()
{
            / * variable definitions   * /
            / * main function body, with declarations of its variables,
            its commands and functions * /

}
```

Preprocessing definitions are commands interpreted by the compiler, at compile time that refer to operations performed by the compiler for code generation. They usually start with a hash sign (#) and are not C language commands, so they will not be treated here in greater detail.

Example:

#include <stdio.h> / * preprocessor command used to tell the compiler to 'paste' the stdio.h file definitions into this file before compiling it * /

Type definitions are definitions of structures or special data types introduced by the user to facilitate data manipulation by the program. Nor will they be dealt with here in greater detail.

Global variable declarations are made when it is necessary to use global variables in the program. The concept of the global variable and the advantages and disadvantages of its use concern the modularization of a C program (see material on modularization and functions).

Prototypes of functions and functions also concern modularization issues.

Main () is the main function of a C program, containing the code that will initially be executed when the program itself is executed. Every C program must contain the main () function, otherwise, an error will be generated during the program generation process (more specifically, in the binding step).

Basic I / O Functions

This section describes some of the basic I / O functions that will initially be used to provide the programmer with a keyboard data input channel and a monitor data output channel.

printf () Function (stdio.h Library)

The printf () function is basically used to send information to the monitor, i.e., to print information. Your prototype is as follows:

    printf (data string and format, var1, var2, ..., varN);

where data string and format are literal data to be displayed on the monitor (for example, any text) plus an optional set of format specifiers (indicated by the% symbol and a character set). These specifiers will determine how the contents of the var1 through varN arguments are displayed.

var1 through varN indicates, in turn, the arguments (variables or constants) whose values will be displayed at the location and format determined by the format specifiers within the data string and format. The number N must be equal to the number of format specifiers provided.

Most used format specifiers:

%W	simple characters (char type)
% d	integer (type int)
%and	scientific notation
% f	floating-point (float type)
% g	% e or% f (shorter)
%O	octal
%s	string
% u	unsigned integer
% x	hexadecimal
% lf	double type

% u	unsigned integer (type unsigned int)
% ld	like long int

Examples:

1)

    int n = 15;
    printf ("The value of n is h% d", n);

/ * displays 'The value of n eh 15'. Note that all contents of the data string and format are displayed literally, except for the% d specifier, which is replaced by the integer value of variable n * /

2)

    char charac = 'A';
    float num = 3.16;
    printf ("The letter is% c and the number is% f", character, num);

/ * displays 'The letter eh A and the number eh 3.16'. In this case, the

    The value replaces % c specifier (first of string)
    of the character variable and the%, f specifier is replaced by the value
    of variable num. It should be noted that the types of specifiers and

variables are compatible * /

scanf () Function   (stdio.h Library)

The scanf function is used to receive data from standard data input. We will assume, for simplicity, that this default input is always the keyboard. The scanf prototype is as follows:

scanf (format string, & var1, & var2,..., & varN);

where the format string contains the format specifiers in sequence and relative to each of the data to be received. For a list of commonly used format specifiers, see printf () Function (stdio.h Library) section.

var1 through varN identify the variables in which the values received by scanf will be stored in the same order as determined by the format specifiers. The number N must be equal to the number of format specifiers provided.

IMPORTANT: The address operator (&) MUST be used in front of variable identifiers. Otherwise, an error occurs. For more details, see the pointer theory.

Examples:

1)

    int t;

printf ("Enter an integer:");
scanf ("% d," & t); / * waits for a type number to be entered int. The number entered is stored in the variable t when the user types ENTER * /

2)

char char1;
int i;
printf ("Enter a comma-separated character and int:");
scanf ("% c,% d", & charac1, & i);

/ * In this case, the format specifiers% c and% d are comma-separated, meaning that the user must enter the values also comma-separated and in the correct order * /

getch () Function (conio.h library)

The getch function is basically used to wait for a user to press a key. The key pressed can be captured by the return value of the function (for more details on return value see function theory).

Because it stops execution until a key is pressed, the getch function can be used at the end of a console program to allow the user to view the output of the program before its window closes.

Example:

printf ("I'm showing a sentence \ n");
printf ("Type any key to exit the program");
getch ();   / * waits here until a key is pressed * /

/ * end of program * /

Note: The getche function works similarly, but displays the typed character on the screen (the name means "get char with echo").

clrscr () Function (conio.h library)

The clrscr function is used to clear the screen (the name means "clear screen").

Control Structures
Simple Command

A command line in C always ends with a semicolon (;)

Examples:

```
x = 443.7;
a = b + c;
printf ("Example");
```

Command Block

Braces ({}) are used to delimit command blocks in a C program. They are most commonly used in grouping statements for execution by conditional and repeating structure clauses.

Conditional Structures

if-else Structure
Format:

```
if  (condition)
    {
```

command block 1

}

else

{

command block 2

}

Condition is any expression that can be evaluated to true ("true") or false ("false"). In the case of expressions that have a numeric value instead of a logical value, if the value is nonzero, the expression is evaluated with a logical value "true," otherwise it is evaluated with the logical value "false."

If the condition has a logical value of "true," command block 1 is executed, if the logical value of the condition is false, command block, 2 is executed. For either block, if it is formed by a single command, the keys are optional.

The if-else structure is similar to a compound conditional structure in which either command block is executed; The else clause, however, is optional, and if it is omitted the structure will function as a simple conditional structure, where a command block (in this case, block 1) is only executed if the condition is true.

Examples:

1)

```
int num;
printf ("Enter a number:");
```

```c
        scanf ("% d", & num);

        if (num <0) / * tests if num is less than zero * /
            {
/ * command block executed if condition is true. In this case, as
printf is a single command the keys could be omitted   * /

                printf ("\ nThe number is less than zero");
            }
        else
        {
                / * command block executed if condition is false.
                In this case, as printf is a single command the keys
                could be omitted   * /

                printf ("\ nThe number is greater than zero");
        }
```

2)

```c
        if ((a == 2) && (b == 5)) / * condition with logical operation
    * /
                printf ("\ nCondition satisfied"); / * command block * /

        getch (); / * this statement is not part of the structure
                conditional, therefore always executed * /
```

3)

```c
        if (m == 3)
```

```
        {
if ((a> = 1) && (a <= 31)) / * this if is part of the previous if
command block * /
            {
                printf ("Date OK");
            }
        else / * this else is from the nearest if (which does
                part of the command block)    * /
            {
                printf ("Invalid Date");
        }
        }
```

Switch Structure

Format:

```
        switch (expression)
        {
                case value1:
                        seq. of commands 1
                        break;
                case value2:
                        seq. of commands 2
                        break;

                . . .
        case valueN:
                        seq. N commands
                        break;
                default:
```

seq. standard

```
    }
```

The switch command evaluates the expression and compares successively against a list of constants value1 to valueN (minus string constants). When it finds a match between the expression value and the constant value, it jumps to the corresponding case clause and executes the associated command sequence until it finds a break statement, then exits the structure.

The default clause is executed if no match is found. This clause is optional and, if not present, no action will be taken if all matches fail. It is typically used to direct any free end that may be pending in the switch statement.

COMMENTS:

1. If the break command is forgotten at the end of a sequence of commands, execution continues for the next case statement until a break or the end of the switch is encountered, which is usually unwanted.

2. never two case constants on the same switch can have equal values.

3. A switch statement is more efficient than an if-else thread, and can be written much more "elegantly."

4. value1 to valueN MUST be constant values.

Examples:

1)

```
int dia;
printf ("Enter a day of the week from 1 to 7");
scanf ("% d", & dia);
switch (day) / * tests the value of the variable day * /
{
    case 1:
printf ("Sunday");
break;
    case 2:
printf ("Monday");
break;
    case 3:
printf ("Tuesday");
break;
    case 4:
printf ("Wednesday");
break;
    case 5:
printf ("Thursday");
break;
    case 6:
printf ("Friday");
break;
    case 7:
printf ("Saturday");
break;
    default:
```

printf ("This day does not exist"); / * only enters here if the user does not enter a day between 1 and 7   * /

break;

}

Repetition Structures

While Structure

Format:

```
while (condition)
{
        command sequence
}
```

The while command evaluates   the   logical condition value; if   the logical value is true (true), the command sequence is executed, otherwise, the program execution continues after the structure while. If the command sequence consists of a single command, the use of keys is optional.

After   the   command   sequence   has   been   executed,   the logical condition value is reevaluated, and if it remains true, the command sequence is executed again. This behavior is repeated until the truth value of the condition is false (false) when the execution of the structure while it is stopped and continued on the next instruction.

Each of the command sequence runs is called a loop iteration. In the case of the while structure, the number of iterations can range from

0 to N, where N is the number of the iteration, after which the condition test results in a false logical value.

NOTE: If the condition is true on the first test and the command sequence is executed, it must make the condition false at some point; otherwise, the condition will always be reevaluated as true, and the command sequence will be executed in an infinite number of iterations.

Example:

```
int x = 0;

/ * prints x values from 0 to 9
the value 10 is not printed because when testing the condition
for
x equals 10, the logical value is false and the while execution
is interrupted   * /

while (x <10)
{
    printf ("\ nx =% d", x);
    x ++; / * makes the condition false
                at any moment */
}
```

do-while Structure

Format:

```
of {
```

command sequence

```
} while (condition);
```

The command sequence is always initially executed in a do-while structure. After its execution, the logical value of the condition is evaluated, and if true, the command sequence is executed again. The cycle is repeated until the truth value of the condition is false (false), where execution continues in the following statement to the structure of the while. If the command sequence consists of a single command, the use of keys is optional.

Unlike in the while structure, in the do-while structure, the number of iterations varies between 1 and N, where N is the number of the iteration, after which the condition test results in a false logical value.

NOTE: As with the while structure, if the condition is true on the first test, the command sequence must make the condition false at some point.

Example:

```
int num;

of {

    printf ("Enter a number from 1 to 9:")
    scanf ("% d", & num);
```

} while (! ((num> = 1) && (num <= 9))); / * in this case, obtaining

of the value of one way

scanf may   make the condition false * /

for Structure

Format:

```
for (initialization; condition; increment)
{
        command sequence
}
```

The initialization is performed only once, at the beginning of the execution of the structure is, and is usually an assignment used to initialize some loop control variables.

After initialization, the logical value of the condition is tested. If true, the command sequence is executed, otherwise, execution continues after the for structure. At the end of the command sequence execution, the command corresponding to the increment is executed, and the condition is retested.

The cycle is repeated until the test condition results in a logical false value (false) when then execution continues after the structure is. If the command sequence consists of a single command, the use of keys is optional.

The for the structure is equivalent to a while structure of the following format:

79

boot
while (condition)
{
        command sequence
        increment
}

COMMENTS:

1. Any of the header clauses (initialization, condition, or increment) can be omitted; In case of omitting initialization or increment, it is considered that these are null commands (that is, they do nothing) while omitting the condition is considered that its logical value is always true. The semicolons that separate each of the clauses cannot be omitted.

2. Initialization and increment clauses can consist of several commands each; In this case, the commands must be separated from each other by commas.

Examples:

1)

/ * in this case x is used as loop control variable
(controls execution between 1 and 100) and also has its value
printed by the printf * / function

for (x = 1; x <= 100; x ++)
    {

```
printf ("% d", x);
}
```

2)

/ *, in this case, the command sequence is null, and the loop is used only to "spend time" counting from 0 to 999 * /

```
for (x = 0; x <1000; x ++);
```

3)

/ * there is no increment, and the loop is executed until the value
entered by the user is 10 * /

```
for (x = 0; x! = 10;)
        scanf ("% d", & x);
```

4)

/ * two variables are initialized, tested and incremented * /

```
for (x = 0, y = 0; x + y <100; x ++, y ++)
        printf ("% d", x + y);
```

Interrupt Commands
Break Command

The break command can be used to interrupt the execution of a loop at any time. Only the innermost loop is broken, and execution continues on the command following that loop.

Example:

```
#include <stdlib.h> / * required to use rand () * /
#include <stdio.h>

void main (void)
{

        int draw = rand (); / * generates a random number
                        between 0 and 32767   * /
        int num, x;
        for (x = 0; x <10; x ++)
        {
                printf ("Try to set the number (between 0 and
32767).");
printf ("You have% d attempts.", 10 - x);
                scanf ("% d", & num);
                if (num == draw) / * hit number * /
                {
                        break; / * breaks the loop (are not
                                more attempts required) * /
                }
        }
}
```

```
/ * if x equals 10, user timed out
unsuccessfully  * /

if (x <10)
{
    printf ("Very good!");
}
else
{
    printf ("Regrettable!");
}
}
```

Continue Command

The continue command works similar to break, except that only the current iteration is interrupted; that is, loop execution continues from the beginning of the next iteration

Example:

```
/ * prints even numbers

for (x = 0; x <100; x ++)
{
    / * if number is not even, go to next iteration
    without printing * /

    if (x% 2! = 0)
```

continues;

    printf ("% d,", x);

}

Modularization in C

Functions

In C there is no distinction between functions and subroutines. That is, all subroutines, from an algorithmic standpoint, can be treated as functions that return no value.

Function declaration format:

Return type function_identifier (type1 param1, type2 param2, ..., typeN paramN)
{
    / * body of the function * /
    return return value ;
} / * end of function * /

Return Type specifies the type of value that will be returned to the caller of the function. When the return type is void, this means that it is a function that behaves like a subroutine; that is, the function does not need to return any value, just to be called.

Examples of return types in function headers:

    int func1 (...) / * returns an integer value * /
    void func2 (...) / * returns no value. Behaves like subroutine * /

The return command is used to perform the function return; This can be used at any point in the function that you want to finish executing and return the value (if the function returns any value) to the caller.

Return Value is the value to be effectively returned and can be either a variable or a constant; In cases where the function returns no value, the return command must be used alone, or you can simply omit it, which will automatically return the function to its end.

Usage examples of return:

return 0; / * returns constant value 0 * /
return var; / * returns the value of the variable 'var' * /
return; / * does not return value. It is used for functions with void type return * /

Parameters param1 through paramN identify the parameters that you want to pass to the function. Each of these parameters becomes a local variable of the type1 to typeN function and is initialized to the value that was passed to you at the time of the function call. Functions that take no value as a parameter must be declared with the word void in parentheses.

Examples of parameter declarations in the function header:

/ * two parameters, one int and one char. The ... refers to any return type * /
... Func1 (int var, char var2)
{

}

... Func2 (void) / * receives no parameter * /
{
}

Example of C function and program that calls it:

int func1 (char charac, integer int, floating float) / * function declaration * /

```
{
    / * one can declare other variables in here, as in a normal
program snippet these variables are local to the function * /
    int other;

/ * use of received variables as parameter * /
    printf ("% c", charac);        printf ("% f", floating);
    scanf ("% d",  & other);

    printf ("% d", integer + other);

    return another one; / * returns the value of the variable 'other'
* /

} / * end of function * /


void main (void) / * main program * /
{
```

char c1;

float f;

int result;

int integer;

/ * this 'integer' variable exists within the scope of the 'main' function, so it has nothing to do with the 'integer' variable that is created in the 'func1' function when passing parameters * /

/ * reads an integer, a character and a float * /
scanf ("% d,% c,% f", & integer, & c1, & f);

/ * call function 'func1' with parameters in correct order * /
result = func1 (c1, integer, f);
printf ("% d", result); / * prints result of function * /

}

Comments:

1. main () is also a function, but special as it represents the starting point for any C program;

2. The result of the function 'func1' in the example above need not necessarily be assigned to a variable (in this case, 'result'); otherwise, the return value of the function will simply be lost. However, as the function was made to return an integer value this should be avoided because it constitutes a bad structuring and use of the function;

3. All variables declared within the body of a function are local to it; that is, they only exist while the function is being executed.

All functions must be "known" wherever they are used, i.e., your statement must come before use. If you do not want to implement the function before where it will be used, you can write a prototype as follows:

Return type function_identifier (type1 param1, type2 param2, ..., typeN paramN);

The prototype must be placed before the function call, signaling to the compiler that that function exists and will be implemented later. In our example, if we wanted to write function 'func1' after function 'main,' we should include a prototype of 'func1' before it.

CAUTION!! The prototype is not exactly the same as the function header; it has one more semicolon at the end!

Global Variables
In C is considered as a global variable, all those variables declared outside the scope of any function (including the function 'main'). Any variable is known only after its declaration, so it is usually declared all global variables at the beginning of the program, before the implementation of the functions that use it.

Example of declaration and use of global variables:

    int c;

```c
char t;
/ * function that returns an integer value and receives no
parameter * /
int func1 (void)
{
/ * there is a t variable that is global, but it works as a local
variable * /
    int t;
/ * c is global, so it can be used within function 'func1' * /
if (c! = 0)
{
        c ++;
        t = c * 2;
/ *, in this case, the value of t returned is that of the local variable
since local definitions override global definitions in the scopes
where they exist * /
        return t;
}
    else   return 0;

}
void main (void)
{
    int return;
    printf ("Enter a character:");
    scanf ("% c", & t);
    printf ("Enter an integer:");
    scanf ("% d", & c); / * tec variables can be used here because
they are global * /
```

```
    return = func1 (); / * call function func1 and return value in
variable 'return' * /
    printf ("\ nResult:% d", return);
}
```

Parameter Passing by Value

In pass by value, a copy of the value of the argument is stored in the called function parameter. Any change to this parameter is not reflected in the original value of the argument.

An alternative to value parameter passing, which is parameter passing by reference using pointers, would allow the function to change the value of the parameter so that this change is reflected in the original value of the argument. This type of parameter passing will be further studied in the chapter on 'Pointers.'

Functions with Parameter Variable List

In C, it is possible to declare functions whose number of parameters is not defined. It is then up to the function, by using specific C library functions, to obtain each of the received parameters and convert it to the desired type.

The cstdarg library provides some data types and functions used to obtain the parameters of a list:

va_list - type of variable parameter list, used to declare a structure (see chapter "Data structures") containing the received variable parameters.

void va_start (va_list list, last) - macro used to initialize the va_list parameter list . Last is the identifier of the last parameter on the right that does not belong to the variable list of parameters.

va_arg type (va_list list, type) - allows, from the list the type va_list, get the kind of value type of the next argument list.

void va_end (va_list list) - finalizes the list parameters.

To declare a variable list function:

Return type function_identifier (type1 param1, type2 param2, ...);

Where the ellipse (...) Denotes the beginning of the variable list of parameters.

An example: a function that takes n values and returns its average:

```
/ * n is the number of values, which are   next in the parameter list
* /
float media (int n, ... )
{
    float sum = 0;
    int i;
    va_list values; / * parameter list * /
    va_start (values, n); / * 'n' is the last fixed parameter before
the variable parameter list * /
    for (i = 0; i <n; i ++)
```

```
    {
    / * here the value of the next float parameter is added to 'sum'
* /
        sum + = va_arg (values, float);
    }
    va_end (values); / * finishes obtaining the parameters * /
    return sum / n;
}
```

Vectors and Matrices

Vector Definition

Vector in C is a variable composed of a data set with the same name (identifier) and individualized by an index.

Vector Declaration in C

The vector is declared as follows:

 type   name [size];

Where type is the type of each of the vector elements and size is the number of vector elements.

To access a vector element the syntax is:

name [index];

IMPORTANT! The index of the first element of a vector is ALWAYS ZERO! Thus, the index can range from 0 to size value - 1.

For example, for the declaration of a vector called test whose data type is char, and that has 4 positions, it states:

char test;

The index of the last indexable element of the vector is 3 because, in C, the first position used is position 0. In this case, the positions available in the vector are as follows:

test [0]
test [1]
test [2]
test [3]

Passing Vector as Parameter to Function

There are three possible ways:

1. return_type name (type v [size], ...);

2. return_type name (type v [], ...);

3. return_type name (type * v, ...);

In all cases the function receives a reference (address). Note that in the last way a pointer is used, which will be explained later.

Because a reference is passed, changes made to the vector elements within the function will be reflected in the original vector values (since its actual memory position will be used).

For example:

```
void exchange (int v [])

    {
        int aux;
        v [0] = v [1];
        v [1] = aux;
    }

    void main (void)
    {
        int nums [2];
        nums [0] = 3;
        nums [1] = 5;
        exchange (nums); / * The argument is the name of the vector
    * /
        / * prints '5, 3' as the nums vector values have been changed
    within the 'change' function * /
        printf ("% d,% d", nums [0], nums [1]);
    }
```

Matrix Statement

The declaration of matrices is as follows:

type name [dim1] [dim2];

Where dim1 and dim2 are the two dimensions of the matrix (in the case of a two-dimensional matrix). To access an array element the syntax is:

name [ind1] [ind2];

Where ind1 and ind2 follow the same rules as the one-dimensional vector indices (that is, they can assume values between 0 and dimension - 1), where ind1 is the row index and ind2 the column index.

The graphical representation of an M 3x2 matrix is as follows:

M [0] [0]	M [0] [1]
M [1] [0]	M [1] [1]
M [2] [0]	M [2] [1]

In memory, it can be viewed as follows (note: left values represent arbitrary memory addresses, considering an array of one-byte char elements):

0100	M [0] [0]

0101	M [0] [1]
0102	M [1] [0]
0103	M [1] [1]
0104	M [2] [0]
0105	M [2] [1]

Passing Array as Parameter to Function

The possibilities are as follows:

return type name (type m [] [dim2], ...)

return type name (type * m, ...)

In the first case, dim2 must be provided so that the compiler can calculate the offset in bytes from the address of the first element for a given position.

In the second case, m can only be used through pointer arithmetic (explained below).

Example:

```
void row_back (int m [] [2])
{
    int aux1, aux2;
    aux1 = m [0] [0];
```

```
        aux2 = m [0] [1];
        m [0] [0] = m [1] [0];
        m [0] [1] = m [1] [1];
        m [1] [0] = aux1;
        m [1] [1] = aux2;
    }
    void main (void)
    {
        int m [2] [2];
        .
        .
        .
        invert_line (m);
        .
        .
        .
    }
```

Initialization of Vectors and Arrays

For vectors: values in braces, separated by commas. For example :

    int cousins [7] = {2, 3, 5, 7, 11, 13, 17};

If the number of initialization values is less than the size of the vector, the remaining positions will be filled with zeros. For example:

    int test [5] = {1, 2, 3}; / * test [3] and test [4] get 0 * /

For arrays, each line is padded with braces, with values separated by commas. All lines are enclosed in braces.

Example:

int m [5] [3] = {{1, 2, 3}}, {3, 2, 1}, {3, 3, 2}, {1, 2, 1} {3, 2, 0}} ;

If any element is not explicit, it will be filled with zero.

Example:

int m2 [3] [4] = {{3,2,5}, {4,6,6}, {1,2,3,4}};

3	2	5th	0
4	6th	0	0
1	2	3	4

Pointers

Pointer in C is a variable that, instead of storing data of a certain type, stores the address of a data of a certain type:

Pointers are often used to:

- Memory mapped I / O access

- Using dynamic memory allocation.

- Alternative to pass by reference parameters (in C ++)

C Pointer Statement

The pointers are declared as follows:

type * name;

Where name is the pointer identifier and type is the data type to which it can point.

Example:

int * d;
short int * ptr;
float * ptr2;

Pointer Operators

Operator &: Referencing operator. Returns the address of a variable. It can be used to initialize a pointer.

Operator *: Dereferencing operator. Returns the contents of the address pointed by a pointer.

Example:

int x, a;
int * ptr;
x = 30;
ptr = & x; / * ptr <- address of x * /

.

.

.

a = * ptr; / * a receives the contents of the given address * /

A didactic way to understand pointers is to "read" the meaning of *
and & as "content of the address pointed to" and "address of",
respectively. For example in the following code:

```
int * ptr;
int x;
x = 10;
* ptr = 3; / * ADDRESS CONTENT POINTED BY ptr gets 3 * /
ptr = & x; / * ptr gets the ADDRESS of x * /
```

Problems Using Pointers

Pointers should always point to addresses corresponding to variables
that have been declared or regions of memory in which no data or
code exists from other programs. For example, the following code
stores the contents of variable x at any address, which may be an
invalid address.

```
int * ptr;
int x = 3;
* ptr = x; /* ERROR! Where does ptr point ??? * /
```

Pointers must point to data of the same type as your declaration,
otherwise, misinterpretation may occur in the dereferencing
operation. For example, the following code does not store the value
56 in variable f, since the floatpointer will attempt to read the size of

a given float from the memory address of variable x and not the size of an int, which is the declared type. of variable x.

```
int x = 56;
float * ptr;
float f;
ptr = & x; / * Pointer to float points to int * /
.

.

.
f = * ptr; /* ERROR! F value is not 56 * /
```

Pointer Arithmetic

Integer numeric values can be added or subtracted from a pointer. The result is an address that follows the rules of pointer arithmetic, that is:

For a pointer declared as follows:

type * ptr;

and initialized with an end1 address :

ptr = end1;

The ptr + N operation , where N is an integer, results in an address that is equal to end1 plus N times the size of the pointed data type (that is, the size in type bytes). For example, assuming variable x was allocated at address 120:

```
int x, y;
int * ptr;
```

ptr = & x; / * ptr receives address 120 * /

y = * (ptr + 4); / * y receives the contents of address 120 + 4 *

(int size) == address 128 * /

Another example:

float * ptr;

ptr = (float *) 100; / * pointer is 'forced' to end. 100 * /

.

.

.

* (ptr + 3) = 15; / * Number 15 is stored at address 100 + 3x4 =

112 * /

Pointer-Vector Relationship

When a vector is declared, the vector identifier marks the start address of the memory area allocated by it. Thus, the vector name can be used as an address reference with the same operators as pointers. Therefore:

int vector [10], b; / * vector allocated at end. 100 (eg) * /

.

.

.

b = vector [3]; / * position 3 == end. 106 of memory * /

Equals:

int vector [10], b; / * vector allocated at end. 100 (eg) * /

/ * In memory this will be stored at position 106 -> 100 + 3 x Size of data type pointed (int = 2 bytes) * /
b = * (vector + 3);

Using a Pointer to Pass Parameters

In many cases, it is interesting for a function to provide more than one output value as its result. But the C language syntax allows only one direct return value (via the return command).

Using pointers creates an alternative for a function to provide more than one output value, based on the fact that the concept of address in a program is scope independent. That is, if a calling function provides the calling function with the addresses of its variables, the called function can receive them in pointers and fill in values at these addresses, which in turn will be available for direct access by the calling function.

Example:

```
/ * function receives two addresses of 'int' as parameters  * /
void exchange (int * a, int * b)
{
int aux;
aux = * a; / * content of address received as parameter * /
* a = * b
* b = aux;
}
void main (void)
{
```

```
    int n1 = 8, n2 = 5;
    / * addresses of n1 and n2 are passed to the swap () function *
/
    exchange (& n1, & n2);
    printf ("% d,% d", n1, n2);
}
```

Strings

String Definition

Strings are miscellaneous strings. They are known as "literals" in structured algorithm theory and are represented in quotation marks. Some examples of strings:

"So-and-so,"
"? Question? ",
"1,234",
"0".

In C, strings are represented by character vectors, ending with the end-of-string character whose value in the ASCII table is zero (0 or \ 0).

String Statement

A vector in C wishing to store a string n characters must be allocated with n + 1 char positions to contain the string terminator. Initialization of a string can be done using a quoted string.

Examples of string declarations:

char phrase [] = "First string"; / * Initialization without dimension * /

char phrase [16] = "First string";

char phrase [6] = {'T', 'e', 's', 't', 'e', 0); / * initialized as a common character array, 'forcing' the terminator character * /

In the case of the first and second example, the vector representation of the phrase string is:

'P'	'r'	'i'	'm'	'and'	'i'	'r'	'The'	"	'f'	'r'	'The'	's'	'and'	0

Where each square represents one byte of memory (one char size).

String Operations

String is not a primitive type of C language, so the following operations are NOT valid:

```
char str1 [10];
char str2 [] = "Word 2";
str1 = str2 / * ERROR! Do not copy str2 to str1 * /
if (str1 == str2) / * ERROR! Does not compare str1 with str2 * /
{
.
.
.
```

}

To operate on strings, functions from the string.h library is used. This library has a few dozen functions with various variations, and for simplicity, only some of the main ones will be explained in this material. For details on other functions, see library documentation (usually available in the development environment help files).

strlen

Prototype:

    int strlen (char * string)

Description: Returns the number of characters in a string (except the end of string character).

Example:

    char name [] = "So-and-so";
    printf ("Name has% d letters", strlen (name));

strcpy

Prototype:

char * strcpy (char * string1, char * string2)

Description: Copies the contents of string2 to string1 and returns the string address.

Example:

char str1 [10];
char str2 [] = "Word";
strcpy (str1, str2); / * Now str1 also contains "Word" * /

strcmp

Prototype:

int strcmp (char * string1, char * string2)

Description: Compares the contents of string1 and string2 character by character and returns

- 0 if string1 = string2

- <0 if string1 <string2

- >0 if string1> string2

Example:

char name1 [] = "so and so"

107

```
char nome2 [] = "Beltrano";
if (strcmp (name1, name2) == 0)
{
printf ("Names are the same");
}
else
{
printf ("Names are different);
}
```

gets

Prototype:

```
void gets (char * string1)
```

Description: Receives a string via keyboard and stores it in string1. Characters are stored until enter is pressed.

Example:

```
char name [10];
gets (name);
```

Comments:

1. the gets () function allows the user to provide more characters than can be stored in the vector, which can cause an error. To avoid this problem, you can use the fgets function:

char name [10];
fgets (name, 10, stdin); / * 'stdin' is a file opened by default, related to data entered via keyboard * /

In the example shown, fgets would take 9 characters (or until the user hit enter) and store the data entered in the string name by adding the string terminator character. It is important to note that if the user typed enter before 9 characters, the newline character ('\ n') would also be stored in the vector.

2. gets () ends when the user enters a space, preventing typing sentences with more than one word. To work around this issue, you can use scanf data pickup options:

scanf ("% s," str); / * Get a string until the first space is inserted * /

scanf ("% [\ n] s," str) / * Receives a string until sent the ASCII character \ n, which corresponds to enter * /

Controlled Data Entry

You can make a controlled data entry (ie characters are checked as soon as they are received) by receiving them one by one. In the following example we will implement a password entry that shows the * characters on the screen instead of the corresponding letters using the getch function (which does not echo the character entered for the monitor). Note that only letters and not numbers and symbols will be accepted.

```
int i = 0; char str [9];
printf ("Enter an eight letter password");
while (i <8)
{
str [i] = getch ();
if (((str [i]> = 'a') && (str [i] <= 'z')) || ((str [i]> = 'A') && (str [i]
<= ' Z '))))
        {
printf ("*");
i ++;
        }
}
```

Dynamic Memory Allocation

Dynamic memory allocation consists of reserving space for on-demand data storage, freeing that space when it is no longer needed. For dynamic allocation, alloc.h library functions are used, the main ones of which will be presented here.

The malloc function is used to try to allocate a contiguous space of n bytes of memory. If it succeeds it returns the start address of the memory area, otherwise it returns zero. The prototype of the function is:

void * malloc (int n);

Example:

```
int * v;
int n;
printf ("How many elements in the vector?");
scanf ("% d", & n);
v = (int *) malloc (n * sizeof (int)); / * Allocate n times the size
of an 'int' * /
if (v == 0)
{
printf ("Error");
}
else
{
/ * here could come the code for vector manipulation

.

.

.

* /
free (v);
}
```

The free () function is called at the end of using dynamically allocated memory space to free this space, allowing it to be used by other dynamic allocation operations. The free prototype is as follows:

void free (void * ptr)

where ptr contains the starting address of the memory area to deallocate.

Chapter 4

Programming with Arduino

To develop your application and put your ideas into practice with Arduino, there is no escape from programming. The writing of the software, but well called in this case "firmware," that is, a program that will be embedded in a microcontroller is the most important step of the project execution.

Once you've done the architecture and designed the wiring layouts for all hardware that will interface with Arduino, the next step is to get your hands dirty and write the code that will run on your board. Let's remind you of the basics of structured languages that are important and give you the conditions to develop your first applications and walk with your own legs. Come on!

What do you Need to Know to Start Programming an Arduino?
Preparing your Setup

The first step in getting started programming Arduino is to download and install the IDE used to write and write the codes on the board. This IDE is open source and is available for Windows,

MAC, and Linux. The download can be done directly on the official page.

Basically, we should perform the following three steps:

1. Power and connect Arduino to PC via USB cable

2. In the IDE, select the board model

    i.   Open the Tools tab, select the Board option and then select Arduino Uno (or any other model you are using)

3. Select serial port to which the card has been assigned

    i.   Open the Tools tab, select the Serial Port option and then select the COMX port, where X is the number the PC has associated with the serial port assigned to Arduino.

After these three steps, the Arduino IDE is ready to use and to write the code on your board.

What Language does Arduino Use?

Arduino's programming language is based on the famous C and C ++ languages , as well as the Wiring language.

The C language is said to be a low-level language, that is, a language that is close to the language of microcontrollers and processors, in which we have to program bit registers, manipulate memory and execute processor instructions. C ++ is already a high-level language; that is, its level of abstraction is higher, and it is closer to human language than to computers. In high-level

114

languages, we do not manipulate memory and hardware resources directly, but rather through libraries and previously available resources that make the language more transparent to the programmer.

The Arduino language uses a number of libraries and features so that the user does not have to manipulate microcontroller bits and registers. From the user's point of view, only function calls and logical procedure writing are used.

If you have already programmed any of these languages, Arduino will not be a problem for you. If you have never programmed in C / C ++, or even any language, there are no problems either! Arduino is very intuitive, and the whole complex part is encapsulated in libraries and functions.

How to Compile and Record a Program

Compiling and recording a program in Arduino is very smooth. First, let's understand what it is to compile a computer program.

Compiling, in the context of programming, means checking all the syntax of the code and, if everything is written within the rules of the language, creating the so-called object code, which is another program, semantically identical to what you wrote, but which is written in microcontroller language. The file generated by the compilation process is exactly the file uploaded to Arduino at the time of writing it.

To compile a program in the Arduino IDE, simply use the shortcut ctrl + R or access the compile command in the Sketch -> Verify / Compile tab.

Now, after compiling a program, we need to record it on our board. To do this, make sure that the card is properly plugged into the USB port of the PC and that it has been recognized by the IDE.

If so, just use the shortcut Ctrl + U, and the code will be uploaded to the board. Or, access the upload command from the File -> Upload tab.

What do you Need to Know to Understand a Program in Arduino?

A computer program has several different components. With Arduino is no different. Like other programming languages, it has variables, functions and routines, logical control structures, and so on. We will understand the main components of an Arduino program in this session.

Components of a Code

Variables

A program variable is a predefined size memory space associated with the type of the created variable. For example, if you need to do a simple arithmetic account in your program, you could create a variable of type Integer named X. So you could write the following line of code:

X = 2+ 3;

The memory space associated with variable X will be filled with the value 5.

Variables can have different types. In Arduino, variables can be of the following types:

- boolean: true or false
- char: one character
- Byte: 8-bit size
- int: 16-bit signed integer
- unsigned int: 16-bit unsigned integer
- long: signed 16-bit integer
- unsigned long: unsigned 16-bit integer
- float: simple precision real number (floating point)
- double: double precision real number (floating point)
- string: string
- void: empty type (no type)

Thus, depending on the mathematical needs and logic characteristics of your program, you will need to declare variables of one type or another.

Value Assignment

Value assignment is the act of assigning to a variable that a value has been created to be stored by it. This is done in Arduino through the "=" sign.

See the examples below:

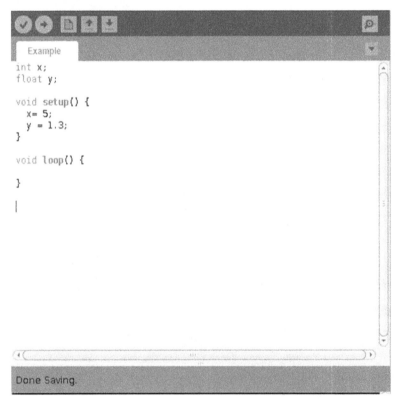

Arduino Variable Declaration.

In the example above, a whole variable name was created X, and a type float variable name Y. Using the assignment signal, we store the value 5 in the X and 1.3 for Y.

Functions and Routines

Functions and routines are separate pieces of code from the main program structure that perform a given task and may or may not return a result. In the classic definition, functions are code snippets that return a value, and routines are functions that return nothing. However, these two names are used interchangeably in everyday life.

For example, if you are writing a program and need to do a calculation of adding some variables several times throughout the code. Instead of writing this calculation multiple times throughout the code, you can create a function named similar (x, y, z) and call that function each time you want to do the math.

The functions have the following syntax:

```
Example §
int x;
float y;

void setup() {
}

void loop() {
}

int somaVar(int x, int y, int z)
{
  return x+y+z;|
}
```

Done Saving.

Declaring Functions with Arduino.

Note that a function is composed of:

- Function Type: This is the type of value the function returns. In our example, the result returned by the function is an integer, so the type of the function will be Int. It is declared before the function name (in red in the example). If the function returns nothing, the type must be Void.

- Function Name: This is the name you will use throughout the code to call the function. It is blue in our example above.

- Function Parameters: Parameters are the values the function receives in order to perform calculations or logical procedures. These values must have a type. In our example, we have three parameters, x, y, and z, of integer type. Parameters are declared in parentheses right after the function name.

- Function Body: In orange, in our example is the function body itself. After the function declaration, the logical procedure you want to write must be enclosed in braces. Between these two keys, you will write the calculation or any task you want to perform with the function.

Flow Control and Decision Making Structures

Throughout your code, you will always need to make decisions, direct the flow of the algorithm and its tasks and calculations, loop to populate vectors, or implement a logical task and various other possibilities.

All of this is done through the flow control structures. We will highlight the top five of them by dividing them into two groups: Decision Making and Flow Control.

Decision Making

If..else

The basic structure for decision making is if..else. As its name suggests, he makes a decision based on a logical assessment. If the result of this evaluation is true, the structure executes code subsequent to if, if the result is false, code follows to else is executed .

The syntax is as follows:
If (logical expression)
   …

      Else
   … ..

Example:

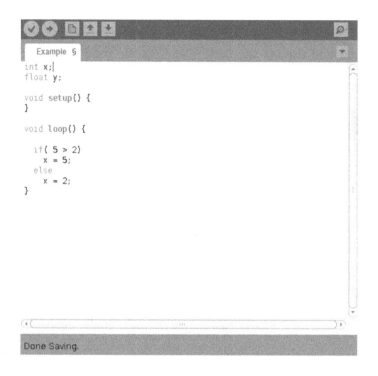

```
Example §
int x;|
float y;

void setup() {
}

void loop() {

  if( 5 > 2)
    x = 5;
  else
    x = 2;
}
```

Done Saving.

Using if… else with Arduino.

In the example above, variable X will be given 5, because the result of the logical expression in parentheses in if is true. If it were false, the value of X would be 2.

There are some variations, such as if… elseif… .else, and also some abbreviated ways of writing the structure. However, if you understand the basic if..else, all other variations will be natural to you.

switch ()

The switch is a decision-making structure that evaluates the value of a control variable and directs the code to a specific case. Let's see what the syntax is like to understand it better.

```
int x;
float y;

void setup() {
}

void loop() {

  switch(x)
  {
    case 1:
      break;

    case 2;
      break;

    default:
  }

}
```

Example §

Done Saving.

Using Arduino switch ().

In the structure shown above, the variable x controls decision making. If the value of x equals 1, the code goes to line Case 1. If x equals 2, Case 1 is ignored, and the code executed is as follows in Case 2. The number of cases is undefined, but it is recommended to be no more than a dozen and no less than three.

In the event that there is no Case corresponding to the value of the control variable, the code executed is Default, usually written at the end of the Switch.

The breaks in the middle of the switch say to the compiler to and out of the switch, continuing the code that comes just below the closing of the keys that define the switch. They are placed after each Case to prevent unnecessary evaluations from being made.

Flux Control

Flow control structures are the famous loops used to iterate and perform tasks. The two main ones are *for* and *while*.

For

The for syntax is as follows:

```
Example §
int x;|

void setup() {
}

void loop() {

  for(i=0; i<15; i++)
  {
    //instruçes
  }

}
```

Done Saving.

Using for with Arduino.

This structure means that the code entered between the keys following the for will be executed x times. That is, if x equals 5, the loop will run 5 iterations. At each iteration, the value of the control variable i is iterated as well. Thus, in the first iteration, the value of i is zero, the second is one, the third is two, and so on until i is equal to or greater than x.

While

While is also a widely used looping structure. The code snippet inserted between the keys following the while is always executed as long as the logical expression is true. The moment the logical expression of while is false, the loop will not be executed anymore.

Example:

While with Arduino.

In the example above, the loop will be iterated fifteen times. Note that when starting While the control variable is zero. And inside while there is a line: i + +. The ++ operator causes the variable to be summed to 1 unit. That is, at each iteration of while, the variable i is summed by 1 unit. Thus, in the first iteration, i starts with zero but is summed by 1 unit and becomes one. In the second iteration, i starts equal to one, is iterated and becomes two. And so on until i equals fifteen. At this point, the while logical expression becomes false, and the while body is no longer executed.

Standard Arduino Code Structure and Libraries

In every Arduino code, you will always find two functions: void setup () and void loop (). In addition to these, you will commonly see lines with the #include directive, which is used to include libraries in code.

Libraries are collections of functions and parameter and variable definitions that instead of being included in the main program, are saved in a separate file and included in the main program through a line of code. Thus, all functions and definitions within these libraries are available in your code. Libraries are very useful as they allow you to split a complex program into more than one file. Library files generally have the extension .h.

The void setup () function is where Arduino microcontroller initializations and configurations are made. The void Loop () function is where we will write our code itself. This is the infinite loop that will run while Arduino is on. All actions in our code should be in this loop.

See the figure below for an example in which two libraries are included, one for working with strings and one for controlling LCDs:

Includes in Arduino.

This default structure, in conjunction with the other concepts you just learned, will be the core code tools of all your Arduino programs.

Continue to learn from reading the next section of this chapter. There we will talk about the hardware interfaces of the Arduino board and how to control and use them in your applications.

Hardware Interface

In the first part of this chapter on how to program Arduino, we covered only software development issues. Functions, libraries, decision structures, and loops, are tools used in your code to implement the logic you need.

But we also have the hardware!

Arduino has a number of libraries and functions ready to access microcontroller settings and manipulate hardware interfaces. It is the existence of these libraries and functions that encapsulate all the complexity of the microcontroller that is largely responsible for the ease of learning and programming Arduino.

Some things end up repeating in every program. Configuring digital and analog I / Os, establishing a serial communication channel, and generating/reading PWM signals are basic concepts you will always need for most of your applications. Thinking about it, let's understand how this is done in this session.

Digital I / Os

The Arduino has 14 digital inputs/outputs. These I / Os are used to read and generate signals of a digital nature, that is, signals that assume only two states: high (5 V / 3.3V) or low (GND).

Before using a digital pin, you must set it as input or output. By default, pins are configured as input, but it is good programming practice to make this explicit in your code.

The functions you will use to configure, read, and set a digital pin are:

void pinMode ()

Used to configure pins as input or output. Its usage syntax is as follows:

pinMode (pin, mode);

Where pin is the digital I / O number you want to configure and mode can be INPUT, INPUT_PULLUP and OUTPUT. For example, to set pin thirteen as a digital output, you would write:

EX: pinMode (13, OUTPUT)

int digitalRead ()

The function used to read the state of a digital pin. In this case, you must have set the pin as an input. The syntax of this function is:

digitalRead (pin);

Where pin is the number of the digital pin, you want to read. For example, if you want to know if pin 13 is high or low, you should write the following line of code:

X = digitalRead (13);

In this case, the variable x must be declared beforehand. It is responsible for receiving the value corresponding to the pin state (1 if it is high level and 0 if it is in GND).

void digitalWrite ()

Finally, the function to write in the pin, or as it is said, "set" the pin to a certain logical level. The usage syntax is as follows:

digitalWrite (pin, value);

The pin is the pin number you want to "set." Value can be HIGH or LOW. So, if you need to set pin 13 to a high logic level (5V), you should write the following:

digitalWrite (13, HIGH);

Remember that to use this function, the pin must be set to output. A classic example of using digital I / Os is led blink; a simple firmware focused on flashing a led. See the program below:

Example: Led Blink

```
modified 8 Sep 2016
by Colby Newman
*/


// the setup function runs once when you press reset or power the
void setup() {
  // initialize digital pin LED_BUILTIN as an output.
  pinMode(13, OUTPUT);
}

// the loop function runs over and over again forever
void loop() {
  digitalWrite(LED_BUILTIN, HIGH);    // turn the LED on (HIGH is t
  delay(1000);                        // wait for a second
  digitalWrite(LED_BUILTIN, LOW);     // turn the LED off by making
  delay(1000);                        // wait for a second
}
```

Example Arduino Led Blink.

In this code, in the initialization function, we set pin 13 as a digital output.

In the infinite loop, the digitalWrite (13, High) function is called, responsible for assigning a high level to pin 13, that is, the led connected to pin 13 is activated. Next is called the delay (1000) function, which pauses the loop for a thousand milliseconds, that is, for one second.

After waiting for this time, the digitalWrite () function is called again, but this time to assign a low logic level to pin 13, i.e. to turn off the LED connected to pin 13. Finally, the delay function (1000) is again call to pause another second.

Analog I / Os

The analog channels are 6. These inputs are used to read analog signals, i.e. signals whose voltage level varies continuously between 0 and VDC (usually 5 or 3.3V).

These inputs are connected to the ATmega328 A / D converter. The A / D converter is an internal circuit to the MCU responsible for converting the analog quantities applied to the inputs into a digital value with which the processor can work. The Arduino UNO A / D converter has a 10-bit resolution. This means that a signal ranging from 0 to VDC in analog terms when converted to digital will be a value ranging from 0 to 1024. Each unit in this range from 0 to 1024 corresponds to VCC / 1024.

If the reference voltage is 5V, each unit in this range from 0 to 1024 will correspond to 4.88 mV.

To work with analog inputs, you will use the following functions:

analogReference (type)

This function is used to set the A / D converter reference voltage. Its syntax is:

analogReference (type);

Which type defines the possible A / D channel settings. Are they:

- **DEFAULT:** The default conversion voltage is the board supply voltage. Usually, these values are 5V or 3.3V

- **INTERNAL:** Internal reference of 1.1V in Atmega168 and Atmega328, and 2.56V in ATmega8;

- **INTERNAL1V1:** 1.1V reference, only on Arduino Mega;

- **INTERNAL2V56:** Internal 5.6 V reference, only on Arduino Mega;

- **EXTERNAL:** Voltage reference applied to the AREF pin (between 0 and 5V).

To configure the A / D converter to operate with external AREF voltage, for example, you must write the following:

analogReference (EXTERNAL);

The other function used is:

int analogRead (pin)

This function is used to read the value of one of the analog inputs. Its syntax is as follows:

SensorValue = analogRead (pin);

SensorValue is any variable to store the value read. The pin parameter is the input number you want to read. For example, if you want to store the value of analog channel 1, you would write:

SensorValue = analogRead (1);

Analog Sensor Example

In the example below, we see how an analog sensor is read. This sensor could be a thermistor to measure temperature, a potentiometer, a light sensor, and any other whose output signal is analog.

```
AnalogInput §

  http://www.arduino.cc/en/Tutorial/AnalogInput
 */

int sensorPin = A0;    // select the input pin for
int ledPin = 13;       // select the pin for the LED
int sensorValue = 0;   // variable to store the value

void setup() {
  pinMode(ledPin, OUTPUT);
  analogReference(DEFAULT);
}

void loop() {
  // read the value from the sensor:
  sensorValue = analogRead(sensorPin);
  // turn the ledPin on
  digitalWrite(ledPin, HIGH);
  // stop the program for <sensorValue> millisecond
  delay(sensorValue);
  // turn the ledPin off:
  digitalWrite(ledPin, LOW);
  // stop the program for for <sensorValue> millise
  delay(sensorValue);
}
```

Compilação terminada.

Analog Sensor Example with Arduino

In the void Setup () function, we set pin 13 as the digital output and the A / D converter reference voltage for DEFAULT, i.e. the board supply voltage.

In the infinite loop, we use the analogRead () function; to read the sensor value, which in this case is located at pin A0 (value 0 could also have been assigned).

After reading the sensor value, pin 13 is activated, and shortly after that a delay whose wait value is the read value of the sensor is called. That is, the hold time depends on the value read from the sensor. After the first delay, pin 1 is deactivated, and a new delay is called.

This program only turns on and off the LED connected to pin 13, varying the waiting time according to the sensor signal.

Serial Communication

Serial communication, known by the acronym UART, is a very interesting feature to make a communication channel between the board and the computer or between the microcontroller and other modules such as GSM, GPS devices, among others.

Here are the main functions for using Arduino UNO serial channel. On the board, you can see that there is a digital pin named RX, and another pin named TX. These are the two pins used in serial communication.

The functions you will use to establish serial communication are:

- **Serial.begin ():** It is used to configure the communication rate and other parameters. It is the first function that should be called

- **Serial.available ():** This function returns the number of bytes available in the read buffer. It can be useful to find out if there is any data in the buffer to read or not.

- **Serial.read ():** Reads the most recent byte of the read buffer.

- **Serial.print ():** Writes a given the word in ASCII code to the serial port.

- **Serial.println ():** Same as above, but it adds at the end of the word a line break character (/ n).

- **Serial.write ():** Writes a byte to the serial port.

The Arduino IDE has a serial terminal that can be used to view receiving and sending data to the board. To access this serial terminal, click the Serial Monitor icon or go to Tools -> Serial Monitor menu.

PWM

The PWM technique, which stands for Pulse Width Modulation, is a technique used to vary the average value of a periodic waveform. The basic idea of PWM is to keep the frequency of a fixed square wave and vary the time the signal is at a high logical level.

That is, the time the signal is activated varies. This time is called the Duty Cycle, and it is by varying this time that the average value can be varied proportionally.

Arduino Uno has specific pins for PWM outputs. These pins are indicated by the '~' character in front of their number. The function used to generate a PWM signal is AnalogWrite, see its syntax below:

analogWrite (Pin_PWM, value);

Pin_PWM corresponding to the pin to which the PWM will be applied. Value is the duty cycle to be applied to the PWM signal. This value must be between 0 and 255, with 0 being a 0% duty cycle and 255 being a 100% Duty Cycle.

Programming

Let's now make an example application for you to train the knowledge gained. This example will be a little different. We will not show any code, because everything you will need, the functions and programming structures, have already been shown in the previous examples.

Here in our example, we will describe the application and just present the logical structure of the program. You are the one who will have to implement in your Arduino by replacing the logical descriptions with the necessary functions and codes, as you learned in this post. So, are you excited ?! To enter the Arduino world, you have to be!

Let's start.

Challenge

Our application is as follows:

"Control the brightness of a led, using as a control signal the ambient temperature. Also, the ambient temperature should be displayed on the computer terminal. "

Description of Application Needs

From the description of our challenge, we know the following:

- We have to control the brightness of a led. This means we have to apply a variable voltage signal to the led terminals. In other words, we have to use a PWM output to vary the activation voltage of the led.

- The brightness of the led should be proportional to the ambient temperature. That is, we will have to read a sensor to know the ambient temperature. This means that we will use one of the analog channels to read the signal from a temperature sensor.

- It is necessary to display on the PC terminal the temperature value read with Arduino. This means that we will have to use the Arduino serial channel to send the read temperature value to the PC and display it on a serial terminal, for example, the Arduino IDE terminal itself.

- From the logical point of view, the problem does not require major elaborations. We basically have to monitor a temperature sensor continuously, and based on the variations that the sensor perceives, we will adjust the Duty Cycle of a PWM applied to an LED and also send the temperature data to the PC via a serial port.

Algorithm

Let's draw an algorithm of what this application would look like. We already know the base structure of every Arduino program, which is the void Setup () and void Loop() functions. In the image below, you can see the walkthrough of how your void Setup () function should look.

Examples:

```
// We have to declare the variables we will use
Step 0: Declarable Variable to Store Sensor Lad ° Value
void setup ()
{
// Here we have to configure and initialize Arduino
```

Step 1: Configure pin 13 (led) for digital output

Step 2: Set the A / D converter to the standard reference voltage

Step 3: Configure Serial Channel Baud Rate

Now the algorithm of what the Void Loop () function should look like.

Example §

```
void loop ()
{
// Here is our application itself
```

Step 1: Read Temperature Sensor Value

Step 2: Knowing the sensor's temperature range, convert the read value using a factor to fit a range from 0 to 100

Step 3: Use the converted value to vary the PWM Duty Cycle applied to pin 13 led

Step 4: Convert the read value from the temperature sensor to an actual temperature value.

Step 5: Send this value to PC using the serial channel

Step 6: Use a delay to regulate the reading frequency of the sensor and also to ensure that serial communication has finished sending data. Writing data on PC and computationally slow operation

```
}
```

So, now it's easy, right ?! Go back to the previous topics of the text, identify which functions to use, and write your code.

Ardublock - Graphic Programming for Arduino

How to Program Arduino with Block Graphics Language

Ardublock is a programming language that uses ready function blocks. Just as Arduino helps enthusiasts get in the middle of electronics and automation, Ardublock helps those with no programming skills to create Arduino programs simply and intuitively.

Since Ardublock's available blocks match the functions of a programming language, Ardublock has a wide range of usability and application.

Installing Ardublock

Once Arduino is configured, go to the Ardublock website to download and install Ardublock on the Arduino IDE:

- Download the file from the website in the DOWNLOADS section.

- Locate where the Arduino Sketchbook is located.

  o In Windows, by default it is found in: "Documents \ Arduino" inside your user's folder;

  o On Mac, by default it is found in "Documents / Arduino" inside your user's folder;

  o On Linux, by default, you can find "sketchbook" in your user's folder.

- Once you find this folder create a subfolder named: tools and inside it another subfolder called ArduBlockTool and yet another subfolder called tool.

- Copy the downloaded file to this last folder.

- Now when you open Arduino IDE, in the tools section, Ardublock will appear in the list. (See figure below).

Programming with Ardublock

Here we will demonstrate how to perform a simple LED flashing program in the Ardublock program environment. On the left of Ardublock are all available functions, from logic operators and state conditions to Arduino input and output controls, etc.

Phases

1. Loop Function

Any Arduino program must contain the loop function. This function is performed indefinitely when Arduino is turned on. So that's where we want to put our blocks.

- Hit the Control section and drag the loop block to the desktop;

2. Setting the LED

To simplify the project, we will use the internal LED, already embedded in Arduino, located on pin 13.

- Push in the Pins section and drag the digital pin set block to the desktop;

This block has 2 arguments: Pin number and desired logical state.

- Push in the Pins section and drag the digital pin set block to the desktop;

- Select pin 13 and high logic level (HIGH);

3. Lead Time

Let's use the delay milliseconds block to make a delay of 1 second. Its parameter is the time delay in milliseconds.

144

- Click on the Utilities section and drag the delay milliseconds block ;

- Set the value to 1000. (Corresponding to 1 second);

4. Connection

Ardublock, like the Arduino language, is sequential so that it will perform one function at a time. To give the instructions of instructions in Ardublock, we connect one function below the other by simply dragging and attaching one pad below the other.

- Do this for the last 2 blocks created. Placing the delay below the digital pin set.

Now, these 2 little blocks form one block. Since we want to turn the LED on for a second and then turn it off for a second, we need a second block of this to do the second operation.

- Right-click on this block and hit the clone button to make a copy.

- Snap the copy of the block created below the original block, and set the second digital pin set to LOW

5. Connection with the loop

This new block now represents what we want to do in the program: Flash the LED at 1-second interval.

- Finally, connect this block inside the loop by dragging it.

- Click the upload button to save the program to your Arduino.

6. Comments

- Make sure in the tools section of the Arduino window that the card and communication port has been selected correctly.

- Ardublock takes care of configuring pin inputs and outputs to make it easier for the user.

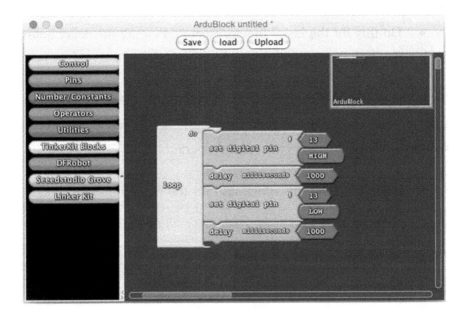

Here we have reached the end of this chapter: Programming with Arduino. At this stage, now we hope that you are confident enough to test your first programming with Arduino.

Chapter 5

Arduino Electrical Scheme

In this chapter, we will explain the entire Arduino UNO R3 version schematic, showing the functions of each component in the circuit. All board components, without exceptions, are explained here. At the end of this chapter, you will understand the basics of each part of the circuit and have a good foundation for better evaluating commercially available Arduino cards, understanding the differences between different models, including compatible clones and cards.

Our goal during the preparation of this material was to pass as much information as possible while maintaining a simple language. The idea is that anyone with any knowledge of electronics and design can understand the material without any major difficulties.

During the explanation, we also made several comparisons of UNO with other versions of Arduino. This will allow you to learn more about the differences between them, and to understand any schematic of the Arduino family better. We hope you will enjoy it and like it.

Arduino UNO Project

Currently, Arduino UNO is the most popular and best-selling version of the entire Arduino line, as well as serving as a base for other models such as the Arduino MEGA 2560, for example. For this reason, we chose him to do this section.

Designs across the official Arduino line are made using Eagle software. There is a free version of Eagle that you can download and use to open or modify the original Arduino designs. The original Arduino UNO project can be downloaded directly from the Arduino website.

Installing Eagle and downloading Arduino project files are optional and are not required to accompany this lesson.

Schematic Analysis

The complete schematic diagram of the Arduino UNO R3 can be seen in the image below.

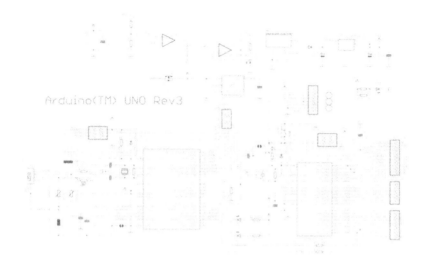

Original Arduino UNO R3 Schematic

This schematic may seem a little intimidating, and even a little confusing at first glance.

For ease of understanding, we have arranged it in the original layout. This was done by just aligning the name and value of the components, and also slightly improving the separation between them. However, no components have been modified, removed, or added, maintaining 100% compatibility.

We also split the components into three main blocks: USB processor, main processor and power. All of them will be explained in the following sections.

The figure below shows the schematic after the organization.

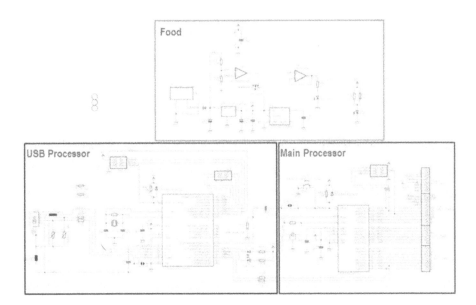

Arduino UNO R3 schematic organized in parts.

Another difficulty that normally occurs when analyzing Arduino operation is the difficulty of locating a specific component on the board since it does not have the identification of all of them. Only the LEDs, connectors, and reset buttons are labeled. Resistors, capacitors, chips, and other components are not identified.

In the figure below, we identify all board components with the same names used in the schematic. You can use it as a guide for locating components.

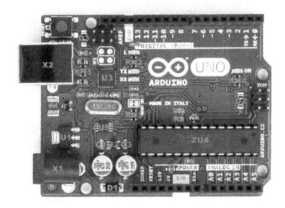

Named Components on Arduino UNO Board

Note the two components marked with a question mark (?). They are on the board but do not appear in the project. This indicates that the project published by the Arduino team is from an earlier version, and not exactly the same as the one being produced. However, we do not notice any other significant differences, and this does not hinder our analysis.

Now enough talk. Let's get down to business, which is the analysis and explanation of the schematic. In the following topics, we will explain how each of the three main blocks works:

- USB processor

- Main processor

- Food

USB Processor

151

The USB processor, named U3 in the schematic, is responsible for communicating Arduino with your PC via the USB port. This is required as the Arduino main processor (ATmega328) does not support a direct connection to a USB port. This way, the USB processor converts the USB data from the PC to a serial signal (UART), which can be read by the main processor. We can then say that the USB processor works as a USB-Serial converter.

The processor used for this function is ATmega16U2. Earlier versions of Arduino, such as Arduino Duemilanove, Diecimila, Nano, MEGA (earlier than R3), and many other similar cards, use another component for this function, the FT232 manufactured by FTDI. However, many users have complained that switching from FT232 to ATmega16U2 has caused Windows and MAC compatibility issues. This way, even today, many "Arduino compatible" cards continue to use FTDI chips.

Let's take a closer look at how the ATmega16U2 USB processor is implemented. The figure below shows the circuit in more detail:

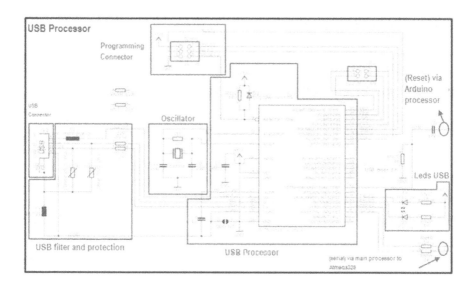

USB processor schematic

USB Connector

On the left, we can see the USB connector named as X2. This is a Type B female USB connector, and this is where you connect the USB cable. Other versions of Arduino use different USB connectors. The Arduino Nano, for example, uses the Mini USB connector, and newer versions like Arduino Leonardo, DUE, and Zero use the Micro USB connector, which is the same as used in most current smartphones.

The USB connector has two functions - bringing information from the PC's USB port to the card, and also feeding Arduino when no external source is connected.

USB Filter and Protection

Leaving the connector, the signals and power from USB pass through the block called "USB filter and protection." We will analyze all the components present in it.

F1

First, all the current coming from the PC's USB port (which will power the Arduino and other circuits) goes through the F1 component. This component is a fuse, and has the function of protecting the PC's USB port in case of a short circuit or accidental overload on the Arduino board. By default, each USB port should be capable of delivering up to 500 milliamps of current, and the fuse is there to protect it if this limit is exceeded.

In fact, this fuse is nothing more than a resistor whose resistance value increases with increasing temperature (also known as PTC or positive temperature coefficient). However, unlike a traditional fuse that blows when overloaded, this component has the ability to reset itself when operating conditions return to normal.

For current values of 500 milliamps or less, the fuse resistance value remains low. In this way, the current flows freely through it (effectively it is as if it is not there). However, when there is a short circuit or overload on the Arduino, the current drained from the USB port increases. This causes more current to pass through the fuse, causing it to heat up and increasing its resistance. Increased resistance cuts the current flow, effectively functioning as a blown a fuse. However, if the short circuit or overload is removed, the fuse cools, and its resistance value lowers back to its original state.

However, it is important to keep in mind that the 500 mA value is just a reference. It is only the minimum required by the USB standard, and many PCs can provide more current than that (in addition to having their own built-in protection mechanisms). So it doesn't necessarily mean that your PC's USB port will be damaged if you drain 501 milliamps of it. The actual current value that effectively "trips" the fuse is not exactly 500 milliamps, but is a function of the time it takes to trip, along with the ambient temperature value.

All versions of Arduino with USB port have this fuse. It is the MF-MSMF050-2 model manufactured by Bourns

Z1 and Z2

USB communication is via the connector pins labeled D- and D +. These signals, after exiting the connector, pass through components Z1 and Z2. They are known as varistors, and have the function of protecting the ATmega16U2 pins against electrostatic discharge, which could cause the processor to burn out or malfunction.

Electrostatic discharges or ESD(electrostatic discharge) are events that occur when approaching an object charged with electrical charges to another that is discharged. The most common example of electrostatic discharge is when you walk on a rug or carpet wearing a rubber-soled shoe, and then take a shock when you try to open the metal door handle. In this case, your body is charged with electrical charges because of the friction of the shoe with the carpet; then these charges are quickly transferred to the door handle, causing you to receive a slight shock. If your body is charged, and instead of the doorknob, you touch an electronic circuit board, loads are transferred to it, which may cause circuit damage (even with the board off).

Electrostatic discharges occur all the time, and in most cases, the current is too low for you to feel a shock, so they end up unnoticed, but can still damage the most sensitive components. Components and circuits with which the end-user has direct contact (as is usually the case with USB ports) deserve special attention about ESD protection, as they normally receive the discharges.

Like the fuse, the varistor is also a resistor, but in this case, the resistance value decreases as the voltage on it increases. At low voltage values, such as occur during normal USB port operation, the resistance of the varistor is quite high (in the order of 100 mega ohms), so the signals pass through them without deviations. However, when an electrostatic discharge event occurs, the voltage increases rapidly (up to several kilovolts), causing the varistor resistance to drop, and diverting excess current from the ATmega16U2 pins to the Arduino GND, protecting the processor.

The component used for this function is CG0603MLC-05E, also manufactured by Bourns.

Arduino versions that use FTDI chips in place of ATmega16U2 usually do not have ESD protection components. This is because these chips already have built-in protection structures, which is sufficient in most cases.

L1

The component called L1 is known as ferrite. Basically, ferrites are used for noise suppression. In this project, its function is to filter out possible noises that may come through the USB cable mesh to Arduino, as well as to isolate the PC from noise generated by Arduino. Not all versions of Arduino have this component, and its presence is not required for operation.

RN3A and RN3D

The last components of this block are the 22 Ohm resistors called RN3A and RN3D. Their nomenclature comes from the fact that in the Arduino design, no individual resistors are used, but components that have 4 resistors together. These components are called a "resistor network" or "resistor network" (RN). Thus, we have, for example, that the component named RN3A is resistor A of resistor network 3, RN3B, is resistor B of this same network, and so on to the fourth resistor (called D). Note that in this case only 2 resistors were used, resistor B and resistor C were left over, and are located just above the filter and shield block.

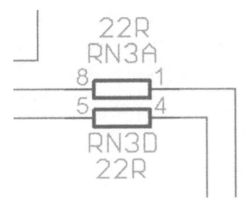

RN3A and RN3D Resistors

The function of these resistors is to attenuate noise and voltage spikes that may come through the USB cable, helping to protect the processor. However, they are not required to function, and versions using FTDI chips do not normally use them.

Oscillator

The oscillator is the heart of any processor and is responsible for generating the clock pulse. Virtually all existing processors use an oscillator, and their implementation is often quite similar. Although it uses few components, the operation of this circuit is relatively complex, so we will not go into detail and focus only on the fundamental features.

In this project, the ATmega16U2 oscillator was implemented using a crystal as its main component (Y1). This crystal has a resonant frequency of 16MHz. The function of the crystal is to generate a sinusoid, which will serve as the basis for the clock. Internally, the processor transforms this sinusoid into a square wave.

In addition to the crystal, there are two 22 PF capacitors (C11 and C9), and a 1 Mega Ohm resistor (R1).

The role of resistor R1 is to facilitate the start of clock generation. Some processors and integrated circuits require this resistor to get the circuit to work after the power are turned on, but this is not required, and its use depends on the chip manufacturer's guidance.

Capacitors C1 and C2 are required in this type of circuit, and in addition to their other functions, have the role of adjusting the crystal frequency. Usually, each crystal has the specification of which capacitor value is optimal for its operation, and it is the designer's role to choose the value accordingly. Wrong capacitor values may alter the resonant frequency of the crystal, or even impede its operation.

USB Processor

This block comprises the USB processor itself, i.e. the ATmega16U2 chip. In this project, he is responsible for receiving data from USB and turning it into serial signals.

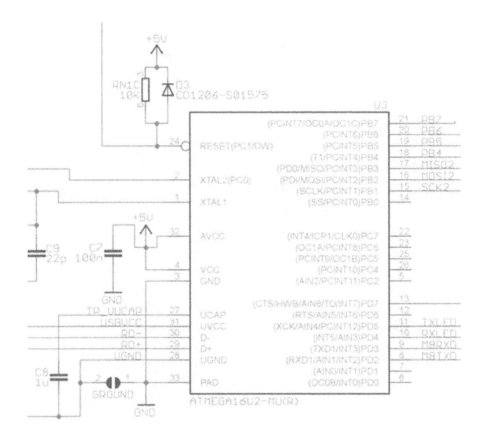

USB Processor Block

C7

We can see the 100 nanoparad C7 capacitors connected directly between the 5 Volt supply voltage and the GND. In this circuit, the capacitor performs the function of the " decoupling capacitor." Capacitors with this function are very important in the operation of digital integrated circuits. Virtually all integrated circuit manufacturers recommend the use of capacitors attached to the power pins, with 100 nanofarad a classical value. In addition to the value, the most important requirement when using a decoupling capacitor is its location and should be positioned as close as possible to the power pins of the integrated circuit in question (if it is removed, its effect will be null).

The main functions of a decoupling capacitor are:

- Filter out the noise coming from the power supply, not letting it get into the integrated circuit. Also, they filter out the noise generated internally in the integrated circuit, not letting it spread to other board components.

- A digital circuit, such as a processor, consumes peak current, which usually coincides with clock pulse transitions. The capacitor has the role of storing enough power to supply the current surges required by the processor.

RN1C

The RN1C resistor acts as a pull-up resistor, and its function is to keep the processor pin 24 at a high level (high level, in this case, means that there is a 5 Volt voltage at the pin). This is the processor reset pin, and it is active at the low logic level, i.e. the processor is reset when the pin voltage is zero. In this way, the resistor holds the voltage at 5 Volts and prevents the processor from resetting improperly. The ATmega16U2 already has an internal pull-up resistor for this pin, and the use of internal resistor is not required but is indicated in environments with high noise levels.

D3

Diode D3 has the role of reinforcing the electrostatic discharge protection (ESD) on pin 24.

But why is the diode placed only on this processor pin, not the others?

Well, the story is a little long, but we can say that processors usually already have internal ESD protection structures, which are comprised of two diodes connected to each pin. However, the reset pin is a special case as it is used during software recording, and some (but not all) programming methods apply 12 Volts to this pin during the process. This fact prevents the ESD protection structure from being fully implemented in the reset pin since the diode would prevent the application of 12 Volts the same. In this way, the chip manufacturer removes one of two internal protection diodes. As the Arduino production does not use the programming methods that require the 12 Volts to be applied to the reset pin, the omitted internal protection diode has been reinserted externally.

The use of this diode is optional and is not present in many versions of Arduino, such as Pro, ProMini, Nano, Duemilanove, MEGA and others.

C8

The ATmega16U2 processor has an internal voltage regulator, which is required for the operation of some of its circuits. For this regulator to work properly, the manufacturer recommends that a capacitor with a value of 1 microfarad be connected to pin 27 of the processor (named as UCAP).

USB LEDs

There are two LEDs, RX and TX, which are controlled by processor software and used to indicate USB communication activity. That is, when there is information sent from Arduino to the PC, the TX LED flashes, and when there is information sent from the PC to Arduino, the RX LED flashes. The implementation of this circuit is very simple and traditional; there is only one resistor in series with each LED (RN2B and RN2C) with the value of 1 kilo Ohms, which has the role of limiting their current.

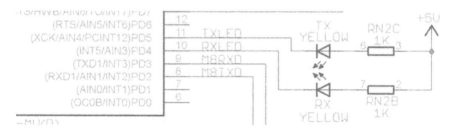

LEDs to indicate USB Bus Activity

Note that since the LEDs are wired directly at the 5 Volt voltage, their activation occurs in an "inverted" mode. That is, the LED goes out with a high logic level on the pin and lights up with a low logic level.

Programming Connector

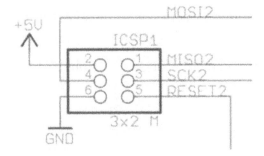

ATmega16U2 Programming Connector

Usually, this connector is used only during Arduino manufacture; at the time, the first software is written to the processsor. This connector is for connecting the Arduino board to the programmer that will record the software (an example of a programmer is AVRISP mkII).

Other Components in the USB Processor

There are still some components attached directly to the ATmega16U2 processor. Let's explain to them now.

RN4A and RN4B

Resistors that interconnect serial between processors.

These two resistors are connected in series with the serial RX and TX signals that go to the ATmega328 main processor, i.e. they are the link between the two processors. The presence of these resistors in series allows you to use Arduino shields that make use of the ATmega328 processor serial. In a way, it's as if the serial coming from the ATmega16U2 processor is disconnected the moment you plug into Arduino, a shield that uses the serial. This brings greater flexibility in the use of Arduino, as it allows the use of serial with other shields, but it is as if the USB port was disabled while there is a serial shield plugged in. Thus, to program Arduino, or to communicate with the PC, it is necessary to unplug the shield that uses the serial.

C5 and RN2D

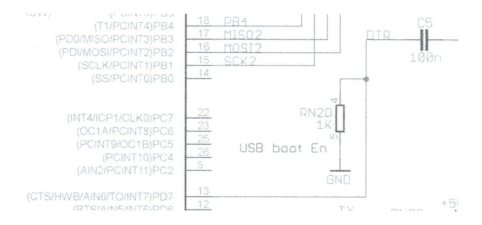

Capacitive coupling on the Reset Line

When you write your software to Arduino, the ATmega16U2 processor sends the information to the main processor (ATmega328) via serial. However, while recording, you must reset the ATmega328 processor to put it into programming mode. ATmega16U2 sends this reset signal to ATmega328 via pin 13.

Capacitor C5 is inserted in series with this signal, making the capacitive coupling between processors. This capacitive coupling causes the reset signal to be sent only for a short time, which is necessary for the ATmega328 to be reset, but to prevent it from being reset all the time.

The RN2D resistor is labeled "USB boot En" and is a pull-down resistor. However, we could not get more information about its function.

JP2

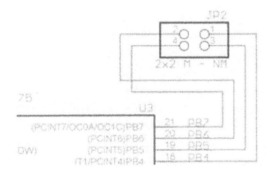

JP2 Connector

It appears to be an expansion connector, but it does not come soldered to the board, and we have no further information about its function.

Ground

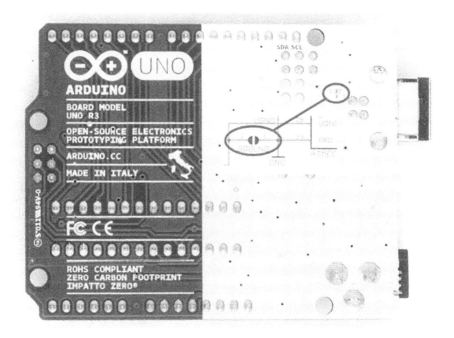

Soldering Jumper

It is a soldering jumper, which is located on the bottom plate. It serves to connect the ground from the USB cable loop (after passing through the L1 inductor) to the main ground. In electronic projects, designers typically make this connection between the "different grounds" using a jumper, as this ensures that they are connected only at one point, which prevents current from circulating in unwanted areas of the board. This jumper is already factory closed.

Main Processor

Now that we understand the operation of the USB processor, it will be much easier to understand how the main processor works, as the circuit implementation is very similar.

As we said earlier, in Arduino UNO, the component that plays the main processor role is ATmega328, also manufactured by Atmel Semiconductor and named as ZU4 in the schematic.

Other Arduino models use different processors. For example, there are versions of Arduino Nano and Duemilanove that use ATmega168, which is basically a component identical to ATmega328 but with less memory. The Arduino MEGA 2560 uses the ATmega2560, which has more pins and more memory than

ATmega328. Arduino Leonardo uses the ATmega32U4 processor, which has features similar to ATmega328, but it has a built-in USB interface, resulting in a single processor board (but this version has not become very popular). Finally, there are also Arduino versions that use ARM processors, such as Arduino DUE (AT91SAM3X8E), and other platforms such as Intel Galileo, which uses an Intel processor (Intel® Quark SoC X1000).

ATmega328 is the "brain" of Arduino UNO, and in short, we can say that it has three functions:

- Receives sends, and interprets serial signals coming from the ATmega16U2 USB processor.

- Runs the software that is programmed into it.

- Interacts directly with shields and external elements, performing device activation and sensor reading.

The figure below shows the main processor block:

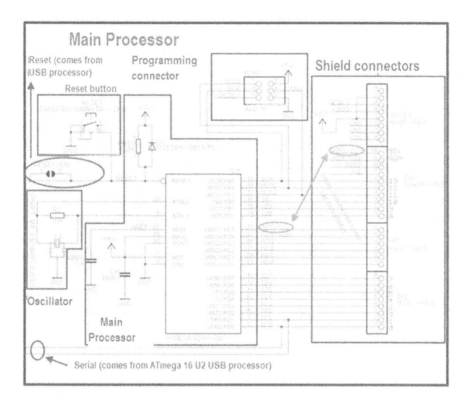

Main Processor Schematic

Let's now take a closer look at how the main processor circuit is implemented.

Oscillator

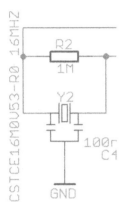

ATmega328 Ceramic Resonator

The ATmega328 oscillator works very similarly to the previously presented ATmega16U2 oscillator, and both have a 16 MHz frequency. The main difference is that the ATmega328 oscillator was made with a ceramic resonator instead of the crystal used in the ATmega16U2.

The ceramic resonator is named Y2 in the schematic, and the model used is the CSTCE16M0V53-R0 manufactured by Murata. Ceramic resonators are components with crystal-like function, i.e. they are also responsible for generating the sine wave that will serve as the basis for the processor clock signal.

Usually, the ceramic resonator is more compact than the crystal, and they come with the adjustment capacitors installed internally, making the circuit simpler. However, in terms of accuracy, the ceramic resonator usually performs worse than the crystal; we can say in general that the resonator has an accuracy of 0.5% against

0.003% of the crystal. That is why resonators are most commonly used in compact and space-saving applications.

Arduino versions like Duemilanove, Diecimila, and MEGA use the crystal as a resonant element. We are not sure what drove this switch to the ceramic resonator in Arduino UNO. It may have been a legacy of the Arduino Nano, as he always used resonators, but it's hard to say for sure.

Anyway, the important thing is to know that the circuit, in general, is the same, only the capacitors are omitted (since they are already inside the resonator), and the 1 Mega Ohm resistor that assists in the start of operation (R2) continues.

Main Processor

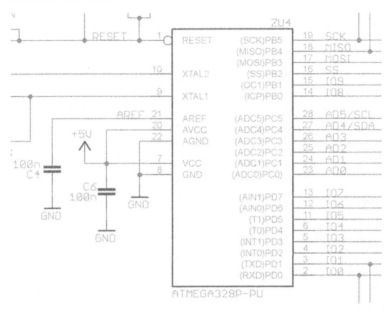

ATMEGA328P-PU

ATmega328 Processor

This is also a block similar to the USB processor. We can see in the schematic the 100 nano Farad components C4 and C6, which perform the function of decoupling capacitors for pins 21 and 20, respectively. The designer could still have placed another capacitor to uncouple pin 7, as recommended, but it was not inserted in this scheme.

The RN1D and D2 components fulfill the pull-up and ESD protection function for the reset pin, similar to the RN1C and D3 components on the USB processor.

We can also notice the serial signals coming from the USB processor, which are connected to pins 2 and 3 of the ATmega328, as well as the reset signal connected to pin 1.

Programming Connector

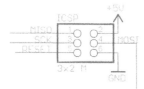

ATmega328 Programming Connector.

This connector, like the USB processor, is used for programming the first software made at the Arduino factory (this software is called bootloader).

Reset button

ATmega328 reset button.

The button is named as RESET in the schematic. When pressed, the button closes the pins 1 and 2 contacts with pins 3 and 4, connecting the processor reset pin directly to the GND. This causes a low logic level on this pin, which resets the processor.

Shield Connectors

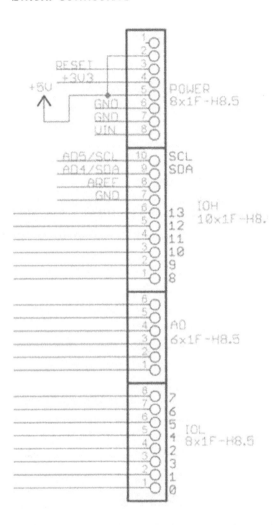

ATmega328 Connectors for Shield Fittings

These are the connectors used to plug the shields into the Arduino. They are connected directly to the processor I / O pins, as well as to the 5V, VIN, 3.3V and GND supply voltages.

Note that in the schematic, all signals with the same name are interconnected, regardless of whether there is a physical connection between them. For example, the two branches named AD5 / SCL are electrically connected, even though there appears to be a "loose" end on the connector (see complete block schematic image), so do the 3.3V, RESET, GND and all others.

Try to match the connectors shown in the schematic with the connectors on the board. Note that they are named as POWER, IOH, AD, and IOL, and the green caption indicates the numbering or function of the pin in Arduino. Also, there is an inscription indicating the size and model of the connector, for example, the caption "8x1F-H8.5" indicates that it is an 8-pin connector, a female-type speaker, and an 8.5mm.

food

Let's move on to the last block of the schematic, and see how the Arduino UNO power supply works.

The figure below shows the components present in this block:

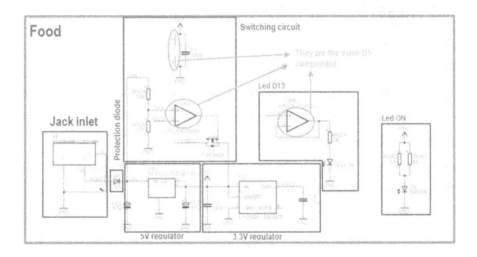

Arduino UNO Power Schematic

Input Jack

This connector, named X1, is where you connect the external power supply plug. It is convenient to use an external source to power the Arduino when it cannot always be plugged into the PC's USB port, when there is an element in the application that needs to be powered with a voltage greater than 5 Volts, or when the circuit requires a current than 500mA supported by the PC's USB port.

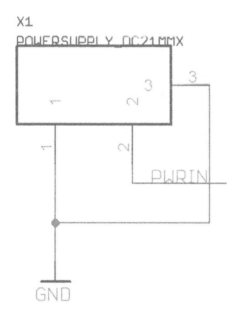

Jack for an External Source

The recommended voltage range for external source Arduino power is 7 to 12 Volts, even though the board supports voltages of up to 20 Volts. The use of voltages greater than 12 Volts may cause overheating of the regulators and is not recommended (we will see more details about this below).

This connector is a female type and set to 2.1 mm, which means the pin in its center is 2.1 mm in diameter. This means that the source used must have a male connector, also with 2.1 mm and positive center (i.e., the inside of the plug has positive voltage compared to the outside, which is the GND).

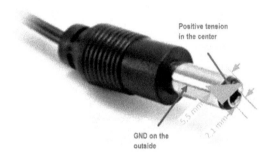

Image of 2.1mm Plug required for Connection to Arduino

Unfortunately, there is no international standard for this type of plug (as there is for USB connectors, for example), so it is not difficult for you to come across a power supply that does not have a proper connector to connect to Arduino.

Protection Diode

The current flowing through the input jack soon encounters the first component, which is the protection diode D1. Its function is to protect the Arduino if an inverted polarity source is accidentally plugged into the jack. An inverted polarity font, in this case, would be a negative center model.

When accidentally connecting a reverse-polarity source to an unprotected electronics board, it causes reverse current to flow, causing multiple components to burn out, destroying most circuits. In the case of Arduino, diode D1 prevents current from flowing backward, protecting the board. Briefly, we can say that the diode functions as a closed switch for correct polarity sources, and as an open switch for reverse polarity sources.

It is important to note that when a reverse polarity source is connected to the Arduino, the Arduino is protected but does not work, and it is necessary to adjust the polarity of the source for normal operation.

After passing through the protection diode, the voltage from the source is called a VIN, and is also available on one of the Arduino connectors.

The diode used is the M7 model, which is the SMD version of the popular 1N4007, and the maximum current supported is 1A. However, the voltage drop on this diode is large, reaching 1.1 Volts, which can bring undesirable effects such as increased thermal dissipation, causing loss of efficiency. In this case, a Schottky diode would be more appropriate because the voltage drop on it is smaller.

Most other versions of Arduino do not specify which diode model was used. Also, some versions like Nano do not have this polarity reversal protection. There are still other versions like Leonardo and Arduino Micro that use other components, or the same diode connected differently. Download the designs of these boards and try to compare the differences in circuits.

5V regulator

The next component of the circuit that we will look at is the 5 Volt regulator named U1. Its function is to lower the source voltage (which can have a value between 7 and 20 Volts) and stabilize it at 5 Volts, which is the recommended voltage for the operation of Arduino components, such as the two processors. In addition, the regulator also acts as a filter, attenuating any noise that may be present in the voltage generated by the power supply.

This regulator is called a linear regulator, and the means it uses to lower the supply voltage is simply to dissipate excess power., throwing it away as heat. For this reason, it has low efficiency and usually gets very hot in some cases. If you power your Arduino with a 12 Volt source, for example, you will only be using 40% of the power supplied by the source, the other 60% being thrown away as heat. This happens with any linear regulator, regardless of manufacturer and model. So don't be alarmed if this component starts to heat up when you use Arduino with an external source as it is there for that. If the board is well designed, the temperature will be within limits tolerated by the component (but will probably be above the limit tolerated by your finger, so be careful).

The more the voltage from the external source increases, the less efficient the operation of the linear regulator becomes. Using a 20V power source, for example, only 25% of the energy is harnessed, with 75% being thrown away as heat. So, whenever possible, use small power supplies such as 9 or 7.5 Volts, for example.

In Arduino UNO, the component used for the 5 Volt regulator is the NCP1117 manufactured by ON Semiconductor, and it uses two capacitors to assist you in this task, PC1 and PC2, both 47uF. These capacitors are important for the proper functioning of the regulator. PC1 helps to stabilize the input voltage from the power supply, and also provides the power to supply any power surges that occur while using the card. The capacitor PC2 has the same stabilizing role but in the output voltage. Also, this capacitor still plays an important role in regulator stability and should be chosen carefully according to the manufacturer's instructions for capacitance and series resistance (this is a parasitic resistance that every capacitor has, it is called ESR). or "

Despite the low efficiency, virtually all versions of Arduino use a linear regulator because they are easy to use, inexpensive and reliable. Some models use the same NCP1117; other versions use different chips. Arduino Duemilanove uses, for example, MC33269D-5.0, while Arduino Nano uses UA78M05. However, the function and operation are always similar. There are still other versions, such as Arduino Due, which does not use a linear regulator to generate the 5 Volt voltage (download the schematic from the Arduino website and try to find out the differences. Tip: the IC used is IC2, model LM2734Y).

3.3 Volt Regulator

The Arduino UNO also has a second regulator, which lowers the 5 Volt voltage from the U1 regulator to a 3.3 Volt voltage. This component is named U2 and is the LP2985 model originally manufactured by National Semiconductor (today this company is part of Texas Instruments).

In the Arduino UNO design, the 3.3 Volt voltage is only used on component U5 (which is part of the circuit switching we will see later), on the other component is powered by it. And why is this regulator present? Typically, the 3.3V voltage is used by users to power other external circuits or shields that use this voltage. Especially the most modern electronic circuits are migrating from the classic voltage of 5 volts to 3.3 volts, is very common today in many devices. This is why it is useful to have this feature available in Arduino.

The implementation of regulator U2 is similar to that of U1. The input capacitor, in this case, is the 100 nano Farad C2, and the output capacitor is the 1 micro Farad C3 (see on the Arduino board that the capacitor C2 is located very far from the U2 regulator, which is not recommended in this case).

Some Arduino versions that use the FT232 chip for the USB-serial converter function, such as Duemilanove, Nano, and MEGA, do not have a second regulator to generate the 3.3V voltage. In this case, it comes from an internal regulator present on the FT232 chip itself. Although the current capacity is reduced (50 milliamperes), it is sufficient for the vast majority of cases.

Switching Circuit

As we have seen before, Arduino can be powered either from an external power supply or directly from the PC's USB port. In cases where Arduino is connected to the USB port, and there is still an external source connected to it, there would be a conflict between them as both would try to power Arduino at the same time. This could cause damage to the power supply, the PC's USB port, and also the Arduino.

The switching circuit has the function of resolving this conflict. It disconnects power from the USB port whenever a power supply is connected to the Arduino. We can then say that the external source will always have a preference to feed the set. This process is transparent to the user, so you can connect and disconnect the power supply even when the card is running (assuming USB has the power to power the entire set).

The components responsible for this function are resistors RN1A, RN1B, transistor T1 and chip U5.

Let's start by explaining how the T1 transistor works (the model is the FDN340P manufactured by Fairchild Semiconductor). Since a complete understanding of this component involves more complex concepts such as silicon doping and PN junctions, let's try to abstract a little, and show it more practically.

Transistor T1 is part of a family of transistors known as MOSFET (in this case, it is a P-channel MOSFET). A MOSFET is a device that has three terminals, one of which is the command terminal (called a gate), and the other two are current-carrying terminals (called drain and source, respectively). Its operation can be described as that of an on and off switch. This way it lets it pass, or cuts the current through the drain and source terminals depending on the command that is sent to it. Briefly, we can say that:

The MOSFET remains off (cutting current between the drain and source terminals) as long as the voltage at its control terminal is at a high logic level.

The MOSFET stays on (letting current flow between the drain and source terminals) as long as the voltage at its control terminal is at a low logic level.

Sending the command to turn transistor T1 on and off is component U5. This component is an operational amp (op-amp). The op-amp is one of the most versatile components in existence, and it is widely used in analog electronic projects, making it possible to make oscillators, filters, buffers, adders, and a host of other applications. However, on the Arduino UNO switching circuit, the op-amp is used as a comparator, and this is how we will analyze it.

The component used is the LMV358, manufactured by several companies like Texas, On Semiconductor, ST, etc ...

A comparator has 2 input terminals, which are called - and +, plus an output terminal. Its function is to compare the voltage present at the terminals - and +, indicating through the output terminal logic level, which of these voltages is the highest. The operation can be described as:

The voltage at the output terminal remains at a high logical level, while the voltage at the terminal + is greater than - terminal voltage.

The voltage at the output terminal remains low logic, while the voltage at the + terminal is less than - terminal voltage.

Let's go back to the schematic now. In it, we can see that the voltage present in the - terminal is the 3.3V voltage itself generated on the U2 regulator. Already the voltage present in the + terminal is the voltage VIN from the external source after passing through the resistive divider formed by resistors RN1A and RN1B. Since both resistors have equal values (10 kilo Ohms in this case), they form a divisor by two, so that the voltage present at the + terminal of the comparator is half the voltage VIN (in fact one would also have to discount the voltage drop over diode D1, but let's ignore that because its influence is low).

When there is only a USB voltage present, VIN is zero since no external source is connected. In this situation, the voltage at the terminal + is less than - terminal voltage, making the comparator output remain at a low logical level. This low logic level is sent directly to the MOSFET command terminal, causing it to turn on and conduct current from the USB port. This allows it to power the entire circuit (in the schematic, the current coming from USB comes from the signal called USB VCC that originates right after passing through fuse F1, remember that signals with the same name are always connected to each other, even if there is no physical connection in the schematic).

However, when a 12 Volt power supply, for example, is connected to the Arduino, there will be a 6 Volt voltage present in the + terminal of the comparator (remember the resistive divisor by two). In this situation, the voltage at the + terminal is greater than - terminal voltage (which is always 3.3V), which makes the comparator output stay at a high logical level. This high logic level is sent directly to the MOSFET command terminal, causing it to shut down and prevent USB current from passing through it, effectively disconnecting power from the USB port. Therefore the current from the external source becomes preferred, and it is the one that feeds the Arduino.

Since the source voltage is always divided by two at the comparator input, the minimum value required for it to be able to turn off the MOSFET is 6.6 Volts. This value is below the recommended minimum limit for external source Arduino power (which is 7 Volts), so the external source will always have a preference.

Still, another component is present in the switching circuit, which is the Farad 100 nano C1 capacitor. In the schematic, it is connected to two "loose" pins just above the U5A comparator, but these pins are part of the same U5 component.

The C1 is connected to the power pins of the op-op is our well-known decoupling capacitor (see USB Processor section "for more details).

LED D13

The next circuit we will look at is the Arduino D13 pin LED, which is named L in the schematic. This is the LED that flashes when we run the Blink example. Actually, this circuit is not part of the power circuit, but we inserted it in this section because it shares the same U5 component of the switching circuit.

This LED has a 1 kilo Ohm RN2A resistor connected in series with it to limit its current, and they are connected directly to the output of another amp op. However, although there are two amp-ops in the schematic (U5A and U5B), both are inserted into the same package, i.e. they are part of the same component.

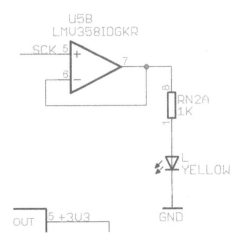

LED Powered by Arduino Pin D13

We have then the + terminal the op-amp is connected to the SCK signal, which comes from the Arduino pin D13, and it is this signal that will make the LED actuate. The – terminal op-amp is connected directly to the output. This amp-op mount is called a voltage follower or buffer. In practice, it does not perform any logic functions as the LED lights up every time there is a high level on pin 13 and goes out every time there is a low logic level. Effectively it is as if the LED were connected directly to this pin.

But then why use the amp-op to trigger the LED?

The op-amp was used because pin D13 does not have the exclusive function of turning the LED on and off. It is also, for example, the SPI communication clock pin (SCK). If the LED were turned on directly, it would drain from pin D13 an approximate current of 3 milliamps while it was on, adding an extra charge. This could influence and impair the use of the D13 pin in other applications.

The op-amp, in turn, has a high impedance on its input pins. This means that the current consumed by them is very small (around 250 nanoamps). This way, it virtually adds no extra charge to the Arduino D13 pin, eliminating the influence of the LED. All in all, you drain from the pin a current of only 250 nanoamps to drive a load of 3 milliamps (12000 times less).

Op-amp is not the only circuit that can be used for this purpose; it is also possible to use buffers or transistors. Another option is to use high brightness LEDs, which are more efficient. This increases the resistor value, reducing the load on the pin, which makes the influence of the LED negligible.

The Arduino Nano does not use this circuit - LED goes directly on the processor pin.

LED ON

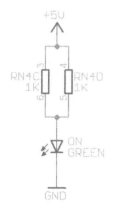

Power Indicator LED

This is the last block we need to analyze, and it is also the simplest. This is the LED that always stays on while Arduino is on, it is named in the schematic as ON.

The circuit has two resistors, RN4C and RN4D, both 1 kilo Ohms and connected in parallel. Effectively they work as a single 500 Ohm resistor and have the role of limiting the current in the LED.

Fiducials

The most attentive may say that there are still missing components to be explained. They are the three circles that appear loose just beside the POWER connector on the original schematic. The figure below shows where they are.

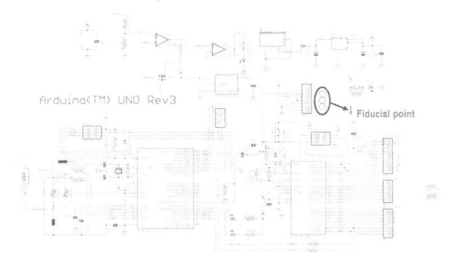

Location of the three circles.

Well, these are not components themselves. They represent some markings on the board and are called fiducial points. These points serve as reference points for machines that automatically assemble components at the Arduino factory, thus achieving better alignment.

In the project published by the Arduino team, there are 3 fiducial points, and they are located below the source input jack, reset button, and ATmega328. This way, you can no longer see them after the components are assembled.

We find another version of Arduino UNO, with the ATmega328 processor in SMD encapsulation, where you can see two fiducial points. They are highlighted in the image below.

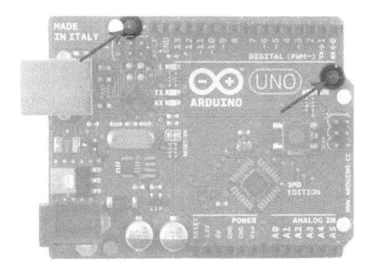

Fiducial Point Examples

We have reached at the end of this chapter and wish your enjoyment throughout the next chapters of the book.

Chapter 6

The LCD Display Function

In this chapter, you will learn:

- Introduction to LCD Displays

- How LCD Display Works

- LCD pinout

- I2C Interface for LCD Displays

- The LCD display with Arduino (4-bit bus)

- Creating Special Characters for the LCD Display

- LCD Display with Arduino (I2C Interface)

Introduction to LCD Displays

LCDs are very useful for those who want to use a microcontroller to develop an application. They allow a simple and easy-to-use visual machine-to-machine (HMI) visual interface. On the LCD, you can send text, numbers, symbols, and even images that can indicate what the microcontroller is doing, the data that may be being collected or transmitted, etc. For those who don't know, LCD stands for English - Liquid Crystal Display- or liquid crystal display. A big advantage of LCDs is that they don't need much power to operate. Remember, digital LCD clocks decades ago? The batteries could last months and even a year. But the LCDs we're talking about have LEDs behind them so they can be used in low or no light environments. These LEDs spend a little more. But if you were to use only LCDs, the power consumption would be very low!

The monitors of the early laptops of the 1980s used the same LCD technology! And without LED lighting.

In the early days of Digital TVs, this LCD technology was also widely used. There are currently other technologies that reproduce images much more faithfully.

The LCD market is always innovating, and today we have color displays: blue, red, green, etc., that is, for all tastes. This Guide will always reference blue LCDs. But be aware that everyone has the same principle of operation. What changes only is the color of the LED that illuminates it.

For the use of microcontrollers such as Arduino, the most common LCDs are 16 × 2 (16 characters x 2 lines) or 20 × 4 (20 characters x 4 lines).

- 16 × 2 blue LCD
- 16 × 2 green LCD
- 20 × 4 blue LCD with I2C
- 20 × 4 green LCD

How LCD Display Works

When they were created decades ago, they were not luminous. They simply let in the light or obstructed it, leaving shadows. The dial is formed of two transparent acrylic plates. Among these plates is liquid crystal. This liquid crystal alters its crystalline behavior, depending on the tension applied between it. The displays, as you can see, are made up of various dots. Each dot may be light or dark, depending on the polarization of the electricity. Under the transparent plates, there is an invisible array of connections that control all these dots. Who does this is the controller chips behind the display.

The most widely used LCD controller chip in the world today is one that was developed by Hitachi - the HD44780, a long time ago. He is so good; he has become a standard. If you want to deepen your study of LCDs by learning how to use all the many features available, I recommend reading the datasheet.

Datasheet HD44780

Communication between the LCD Controller and the Microcontroller (for example, Arduino) can be parallel (4 or 8 bits) or serial (I2C). For a limited number of digital ports, we recommend using the I2C interface.

As a curiosity, be aware that this chip has an internal ROM where some characters and symbols are already engraved. And for you to generate your own symbols, there is an internal RAM. Very versatile!

Here's a part of the internally recorded Character Table - each character is made up of a 5 x 8 dot matrix:

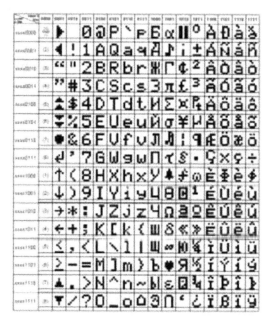

LCD pinout

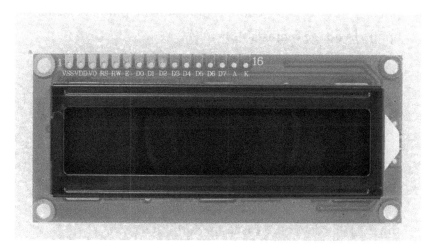

16 × 2 blue LCD display

This is a very detailed Datasheet of a 16 × 2 LCD Display. Note that it uses HD44780 compatible controller chips:

16 × 2 LCD Datasheet

At the top of the display are 16 holes where pins or cables for communication and power can be soldered. Caution: Incorrect connection or use of voltages above 5V may damage the display.

NOTE: The 16 × 2 LCD pinout is identical to the 20 × 4 LCD!

Pinout and Function of each Pin

- pin 1 - **VSS** - Power pin (zero volts - GND)

- pin 2 - **VDD** - + 5V power pin

- pin 3 - **VO** - LCD contrast adjustment pin - depends on applied voltage (adjustable)

- pin 4 - **RS** - Command Selection (level 0) or Data (level 1)

- pin 5 - **R / W** - Read (level 1) / Write (level - 0)

- pin 6 - **E** - Enable (Enables display with level 1 or Disables with level 0)

- pin 7 - **D0** - data bit 0 (used on 8-bit interface)

- pin 8 - **D1** - data bit 1 (used on 8-bit interface)

196

- pin 9 - **D2** - data bit 2 (used on 8-bit interface)

- pin 10 - **D3** - data bit 3 (used on 8-bit interface)

- pin 11 - **D4** - data bit 4 (used on 4 and 8-bit interface)

- pin 12 - **D5** - data bit 5 (used on 4 and 8-bit interface)

- pin 13 - **D6** - data bit 6 (used on 4 and 8-bit interface)

- pin 14 - **D7** - data bit 7 (used on 4 and 8-bit interface)

- pin 15 - **A** - LED Illumination Anode (+ 5V DC)

- pin 16 - **K** - LED Illumination Cathode (GND)

LCD illumination is done by LED. Pin 15 (LED Anode) can be connected directly to +5 V, and pin 16 (LED Cathode) must be connected to ground (GND). This way, the LED will consume approximately 22 mA. The total current draw (LCD + LED) of the 16 × 2 Blue LCD is approximately 23 mA.

If you want to consume less current, use a series resistor, for example, 220 ohms (7.6 mA consumption).

For LCD contrast adjustment, the voltage on pin 3 (VO) must be adjusted. Use a 20K ohm potentiometer. At the ends of the POT connect + 5V and GND. Center pin connect to LCD pin 3. On my blue 16 × 2 LCD, the VO voltage was approximately 1.0 Volts.

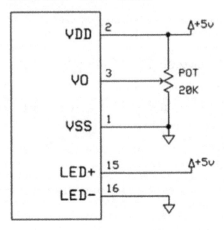

DISPLAY LCD 16X2

I2C Interface for LCD Displays

When this type of LCD Display was developed, the microcontroller data buses used 8 bits. In the Arduino era, the available digital ports are reduced. To address this limitation, a specially dedicated I2C interface for LCDs has been developed. The chip used in this module is the *PCF8574*. It is a parallel port expander, has an I2C interface, and can control up to 8 bits either as input or output (depending on configuration). I2C interface speed is limited to 100 kHz. The supply voltage can be either 3.3V or 5V, which enables it for all common microcontrollers.

This photo is the back of the LCD Display with the I2C Interface already connected.

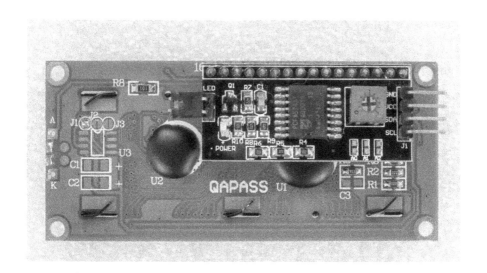

16 × 2 LCD with I2C Interface.

To connect with Arduino or another Micro-controller, only four pins are required:

- **GND** - Plug into Arduino Ground

- **VDC** - connect to 5V power

- **SDA** - Serial Data - I2C Interface

- **SCL** - Serial Clock - I2C Interface

The **Blue potentiometer** on this interface is used for contrast adjustment. After the display is energized and programmed, adjust it to make the image visible. The **LED jumper** is used to activate the Backlight LED. If you do not want to use the LED to save power, remove this jumper. The **red LED** on the board is an indication that it is energized.

PCF8574 Addressing

On an I2C interface, communication is serial. To select a device, the address is sent to the bus because on the same bus, you can have multiple devices.

The PCF8574 chip has some addresses already defined, depending on the model (identify your module chip):

- PCF8574 = 0x20H

- PCF8574A = 0x38H

In addition to the basic address, through 3 address pins (A0, A1, and A2), the addressing can be changed, as in the case of using more than one chip on the same bus. See on the module jumpers A0, A1 and A2.

PCF8574 and PCF8574A I^{2}C-Bus Slave Address Map

INPUTS			PCF8574 I^{2}C-Bus	PCF8574A I^{2}C-Bus
A2	A1	A0	Slave Address	Slave Address
L	L	L	20 (hexadecimal)	38 (hexadecimal)
L	L	H	21 (hexadecimal)	39 (hexadecimal)
L	H	L	22 (hexadecimal)	3A (hexadecimal)
L	H	H	23 (hexadecimal)	3B (hexadecimal)
H	L	L	24 (hexadecimal)	3C (hexadecimal)
H	L	H	25 (hexadecimal)	3D (hexadecimal)
H	H	L	26 (hexadecimal)	3E (hexadecimal)
H	H	H	27 (hexadecimal)	3F (hexadecimal)

One more very important detail! For the I2C interface to function properly, PULL UP resistors must be used on both lines (SCL and SDA). These resistors connect these lines to the VCC. In this I2C module, these PULL-UP resistors (4.7 K ohms) already exist. So do not add any more resistors on the interface.

The LCD Display with Arduino (4-bit bus)

As I said, the LCD Display can be connected to the Arduino via a **Parallel** or **Serial** bus (using the I2C module).

In the case of a parallel bus for Arduino, only 4 data bits are used. But for control lines, more ports are needed (RS, R / W, and ENABLE). Adding a total of 7 doors! This type of communication should be avoided if there is no number of ports available for the application.

This is the **Fritzing** circuit diagram for testing the **16 × 2 LCD Display with Arduino Nano**:

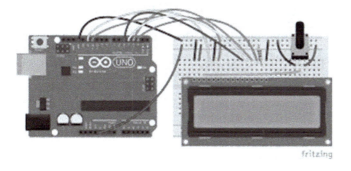

And this is the electronic diagram of the same circuit - Arduino Nano with 16 × 2 LCD:

Note that pin 5 (R / W) is grounded (level zero). Therefore the display can only receive data (write)

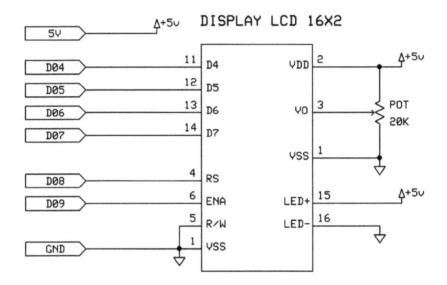

To position characters on display, there is this row and column addressing. See that the count starts from 0 and not from 1 (Row 0, column 0)! The differences from a 16 × 2 display to a 20 × 4 display are the number of characters and the addressing. All commands are identical for both types of displays.

Addressing rows and columns

Columns						LCD 16X2									
Line 0	00	01	02	03	04	05	06	07	08	09	10	11	12	13	14	15
Line 1	00	01	02	03	04	05	06	07	08	09	10	11	12	13	14	15

Columns

Addressing rows and columns

		Columns										LCD 20X4									
Line	0	00	01	02	03	04	05	06	07	08	09	10	11	12	13	14	15	16	17	18	19
Line	1	00	01	02	03	04	05	06	07	08	09	10	11	12	13	14	15	16	17	18	19
Line	2	00	01	02	03	04	05	06	07	08	09	10	11	12	13	14	15	16	17	18	19
Line	3	00	01	02	03	04	05	06	07	08	09	10	11	12	13	14	15	16	17	18	19

Columns

In this assembly, we will use the *Liquid Crystal Library*, so it must be installed using the procedure below.

Installing a New Library in Arduino IDE

To install the new Library, **click Sketch> Add Library> Manage Libraries**.

After opening the **Library Manager** window, refine the search by entering the library name. In the selected library, click **More Info** and then **Install**. After a few seconds, it will be automatically installed. Remember that your computer needs to be connected to the internet. After installing the library, you must close and reopen the **Arduino IDE** program.

Using examples from the *Liquid Crystal Library*, I did this Sketch to test various Display functions:

print message
flash message
cursor test

message scroll test

message direction test

To configure Display Type:

lcd.begin (16.2);   // setting the LCD - 16 columns and 2 rows

lcd.begin (20,4);   // setting the LCD - 20 columns and 4 rows

LCD Test Program

```
/ * LCD Test Program
  ABC Blog - http://blog.abc.com/xyz/
  Arduino Nano - 16/2 Blue LCD - IDE 1.8.5
  Alex Nulsen April 11, 2018
  LiquidCrystal Library https://github.com/arduino-
libraries/LiquidCrystal
* /

#include <LiquidCrystal.h> // Using the LiquidCrystal Library

const int rs = 8, en = 9, d4 = 4, d5 = 5, d6 = 6, d7 = 7; // display
pin definition
LiquidCrystal lcd (rs, en, d4, d5, d6, d7); // setting the pins
int thisChar = 0;

void setup ()
{
  lcd.begin (16.2); // setting the LCD - 16 columns and 2 rows
}
```

```
void Hello () // printing message
{
  lcd.setCursor (0.0); // selecting column 0 and row 0
  lcd.print ("ELETROGATE Blog"); // print of message
  lcd.setCursor (2,1); // selecting column 2 and row 1
  lcd.print ("LCD Guide"); // Print of message
  delay (1000); // 1 second delay
}


void Flash ()
{
  lcd.noDisplay (); // turn off display
  delay (1000); // half a second delay
  lcd.display (); // turn on display
  delay (1000); // half a second delay
  lcd.clear (); // clear the screen
  delay (1000); // 1 second delay
}


void Blink () // cursor test
{
  lcd.noBlink (); // delete cursor
  delay (1000); // 1 second delay
  lcd.blink (); // light cursor
  delay (1000); // 1 second delay
  lcd.clear (); // clear the screen
  delay (1000); // 1 second delay
}
```

```
void AutoScroll () // message scroll test
{
  lcd.setCursor (16,1); // selecting column 16 and row 1
  lcd.autoscroll (); // set automatic message scrolling
  for (thisChar = 0; thisChar <10; thisChar ++) // print from 0 to 9
  {
    lcd.print (thisChar); // print the number
    delay (350); // 350 ms delay
  }
  lcd.noAutoscroll (); // turn off auto-scroll
  lcd.clear (); // clear the screen
  delay (1000); // 1 second delay
}


void dirText () // message direction test
{
  lcd.clear (); // clear the screen
  lcd.cursor (); // turn on the cursor
  lcd.setCursor (10,0); // selecting column 10 and row 1
  for (thisChar = 1; thisChar <10; thisChar ++) // print from 1 to 9
  {
    lcd.rightToLeft (); // print from right to left
    lcd.print (thisChar); // print the number
    delay (350); // 350 ms delay
  }
  for (thisChar = 1; thisChar <10; thisChar ++) // print from 1 to 9
  {
    lcd.leftToRight (); // print from left to right
    lcd.print (thisChar); // print the number
```

```
    delay (350); // 350 ms delay
  }
  lcd.noCursor (); // turn off the cursor
}

void loop ()
{
  Hello (); // printing message
  Flash (); // flashing message
  Blink (); // cursor test
  AutoScroll (); // message scroll test
  dirText (); // message direction test
  delay (1000); // 1 second delay
}
```

Creating Special Characters for the LCD Display

Another great feature of *the Liquid Crystal Library*: create special characters! This library has a method that allows, by controlling the 5×8 matrix points of each LCD character, the creation of any symbol or special character. Use the Link Character Generator below to create Sketch code. To draw, click on the 5×8 matrix points. Copy the generated code and insert it into Sketch.

Custom Character Generator for HD44780 LCD Modules

Click pixels to generate output.

Pixels	Output

```
byte customChar[8] = {
        0b00000,
        0b11011,
        0b11011,
        0b00100,
        0b00100,
        0b10001,
        0b01110,
        0b00000
};
```

Clear | Invert

LCD16x2_Arduino_Caracter:

/ * LCD Character Generator Program

ABC Blog - http://blog.abc.com/xyz/

Arduino Nano - 16/2 Blue LCD - IDE 1.8.5

Alex Nulsen April 12, 2018

LiquidCrystal Library https://github.com/arduino-libraries/LiquidCrystal

* /

#include <LiquidCrystal.h> // Using the LiquidCrystal Library

```
const int rs = 8, en = 9, d4 = 4, d5 = 5, d6 = 6, d7 = 7; // display
pin definition
LiquidCrystal lcd (rs, en, d4, d5, d6, d7); // setting the pins

byte customChar [8] = // Special Character Matrix
{
  0b00000,
  0b11011,
  0b11011,
  0b00100,
  0b00100,
  0b10001,
  0b01110,
  0b00000
};

void setup () // up to 8 special characters can be created
{
  lcd.clear (); // clear the screen
  lcd.createChar (1, customChar); // creating special character 1
  lcd.begin (16.2); // setting the LCD - 16 columns and 2 rows
  lcd.write ((byte) 1); // printing the special character 1
}

void loop ()
{
}
```

I found on Youtube, this application also very interesting to use large numbers on the 16 × 2 LCD Display.

Big Crystal Library

The Liquid Crystal library is very versatile! Allows the use of various interface types:

4-bit parallel interface

I2C Serial Interface

SPI interface

As a reference for reference, this is the link to use the SPI interface (little used):

LCD16x2 with SPI Interface – ARDUINO

LCD Display with Arduino (I2C Interface)

As I mentioned earlier, there is an I2C Interface module specially designed for the use of LCD Displays. The big advantage is the reduced number of ports used on Arduino - only two - SCL and SDA.

Arduino - Wire / I2C Library

I2C Port Connections (for Arduino):

SCL port = pin A5

SDA port = A4 pin

Do not forget to connect the **GND** of the I2C interface in **GND** Arduino. Same for **5V**. The current draw measured by me was **27.5 mA**. Make the **adjustment of the contrast** using the pot I2C interface.

This is the **Fritzing** circuit diagram for testing the **16 × 2 LCD Display (I2C Interface) with Arduino Nano**:

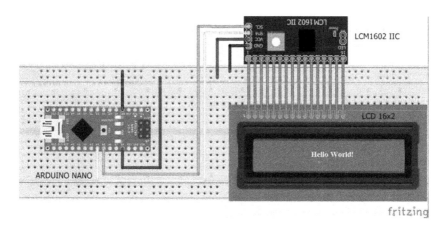

This is the electronic diagram of the same circuit - 16 × 2 LCD Display (I2C Interface) with Arduino Nano:

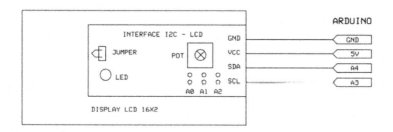

I2C Scanner

The first test to be done is to identify the interface I2C address. Run Sketch I2C Scanner. In my assembly, the address found was:

I2C scanner. Searching…

I2C Address found: 63 (0x3F)   - This address should be entered in Test Sketch

Found 1 device (s).

I2C Scanner

```
// I2C Scanner
// Written by Nick Gammon
// Date: 20th April 2011

#include <Wire.h>

void setup ()
{
  Serial.Begin (9600);
  // while (! Serial)
  {
  }

  Serial.println ();
  Serial.println ("I2C scanner. Searching ...");
  byte count = 0;
```

```
Wire.begin ();
for (byte i = 8; i <120; i ++)
{
  Wire.beginTransmission (i);
  if (Wire.endTransmission () == 0)
   {
    Serial.print ("I2C Address Found:");
    Serial.print (i, DEC);
    Serial.print ("(0x");
    Serial.print (i, HEX);
    Serial.println (")");
    count ++;
    delay (1);
   }
}
Serial.print ("Found");
Serial.print (count, DEC);
Serial.println ("device (s).");
}

void loop () {}
```

This is the **Liquid Crystal I2C** Library used in this test assembly (install it using the procedure above):

Liquid Crystal I2C Library

Using the **Liquid Crystal I2C** Library, I created the program to test the same functions as the previous example (4-bit interface):

print message

flash message

cursor test

message scroll test

message direction test

LCD Test Program

```
/ * LCD Test Program - Interafce I2C
   ABC Blog - http://blog.abc.com/xyz/
   Arduino Nano - 16/2 Blue LCD - IDE 1.8.5
   Alex Nulsen April 13, 2018
   LiquidCrystal Library
https://github.com/marcoschwartz/LiquidCrystal_I2C
* /


#include <Wire.h> // using the Wire library
#include <LiquidCrystal_I2C.h> // using the LiquidCrystal I2C
library
LiquidCrystal_I2C lcd (0x3F, 16, 2); // Set up I2C address and 16
character, 2 line display
int thisChar = 0;
void setup ()
{
  lcd.init (); // initialize LCD
  lcd.backlight (); // enable backlight led
}
```

```
void Hello () // printing message
{
  lcd.setCursor (0.0); // selecting column 0 and row 0
  lcd.print ("ELETROGATE Blog"); // print of message
  lcd.setCursor (2,1); // selecting column 2 and row 1
  lcd.print ("LCD Guide"); // Print of message
  delay (1000); // 1 second delay
}

void Flash ()
{
  lcd.noDisplay (); // turn off display
  delay (1000); // half a second delay
  lcd.display (); // turn on display
  delay (1000); // half a second delay
  lcd.clear (); // clear the screen
  delay (1000); // 1 second delay
}

void Blink () // cursor test
{
  lcd.noBlink (); // delete cursor
  delay (1000); // 1 second delay
  lcd.blink (); // light cursor
  delay (1000); // 1 second delay
  lcd.clear (); // clear the screen
  delay (1000); // 1 second delay
}
```

```
void AutoScroll () // message scroll test
{
  lcd.setCursor (16,1); // selecting column 16 and row 1
  lcd.autoscroll (); // set automatic message scrolling
  for (thisChar = 0; thisChar <10; thisChar ++) // print from 0 to 9
  {
    lcd.print (thisChar); // print the number
    delay (350); // 350 ms delay
  }
  lcd.noAutoscroll (); // turn off auto-scroll
  lcd.clear (); // clear the screen
  delay (1000); // 1 second delay
}


void dirText () // message direction test
{
  lcd.clear (); // clear the screen
  lcd.cursor (); // turn on the cursor
  lcd.setCursor (10,0); // selecting column 10 and row 1
  for (thisChar = 1; thisChar <10; thisChar ++) // print from 1 to 9
  {
    lcd.rightToLeft (); // print from right to left
    lcd.print (thisChar); // print the number
    delay (350); // 350 ms delay
  }
  for (thisChar = 1; thisChar <10; thisChar ++) // print from 1 to 9
  {
    lcd.leftToRight (); // print from left to right
    lcd.print (thisChar); // print the number
```

```
    delay (350); // 350 ms delay
  }
  lcd.noCursor (); // turn off the cursor
}

void loop ()
{
  Hello (); // printing message
  Flash (); // flashing message
  Blink (); // cursor test
  AutoScroll (); // message scroll test
  dirText (); // message direction test
  delay (1000); // 1 second delay
}
```

Conclusion

Have you thought about having a tech-house? One that can offer all the possibilities of Arduino home automation that the market offers? Well, unless you are Iron Man and enlisted by the help of JARVIS (Iron Man computer), this will not be entirely possible at the moment, but with the help of our smart little superhero ARDUINO, you will be able to reproduce many things in your home that you only see in movies.

To conclude this book, we will present 5 Arduino project ideas that you can employ on your home premises, allowing the home automation world to invade every room, controlling and monitoring your safety and day-to-day tasks. Do everything, right!).

This great little microcontroller, which is responsible for the different possibilities of the projects presented below.

If you have your Arduino, then it's time to get it off the shelf and dust it off to get it to work (we're all guilty of it sometimes, don't you think?). Let's add some modules, sensors, a little of our time, and achieve extraordinary feats.

Ready !? Fasten your seat belts and come on!

1- Arduino Design Lighting Control by Cellphone

One of the most coveted projects for technology lovers is Arduino home automation, where you can, through apps, run the house as a whole, letting you open and close motorized curtains and windows, turn televisions on and off at preset times, run fans and everything else you think of, right on your phone, tablet or computer.

Great things in automation can be done by adding an Ethernet Shield to the Arduino, allowing you to turn the small microcontroller into an Internet-capable device that can change the state of lights, TVs, coffee machines - just about anything you can think of - on and off using a browser-based interface or a timer.

Have you thought, for example, about waking up in the morning and the coffee being ready, your TV on and tuned to your favorite channel, because in the Arduino world, everything possible is just a matter of having the necessary accessories and making the right programming.

There is not much secret in the items needed for this; you will basically need 1 Arduino, 1 Ethernet Shield or 1 Wifi Module, 1 Relay Module, LEDs and jumpers. You can also give these commands directly from your smartphone via Bluetooth.

2 - Arduino Design RFID Access Control

How about replacing the old key with an RFID tag to access your home? With an Arduino and an RFID Kit, you and your family members can open doors quickly, simply and very safely, simply by swiping the card in front of the RFID reader to release the electronic door lock or lock.

RFID technology uses radio waves for communication and data transfer, where a unique numbered tag (code) is embedded in a card or key chain, for example, and when passing the encoded object in front of the reader, it will receive information from the cardholder, where permitted, will release the door lock giving access to the room.

The registration of the cards or tags that will be previously allowed to pass is configured and saved directly in Arduino, which is responsible for comparing the information, as well as managing the reading and command procedure for opening the door by activating a relay, which consequently will release the electric lock.

Of course, it is not enough to connect the Arduino and RFID reader for you to be able to carry out this project, it is necessary that the door has previously some kind of electric lock, which will be interconnected to the programming set, executing the received commands.

For execution, you will need 1 Arduino, 1 RC522 RFID Kit (which includes RFID Reader and two tags, one in keychain format and one in card format), 1 relay module, 1 16×2 display, 1 lock or electric lock and jumpers.

This type of home automation is not limited to door use but can be applied to gates, drawers, cabinets, and anything else you can imagine, just use creativity and put it into practice. For more details on this project, go to the "Arduino RFID Access Control Project."

3 - Intelligent Security Alarm Design with Arduino

For those looking for extra protection and not wanting to afford the high purchase and monthly payment costs of modern and sophisticated alarm systems, the little Arduino can be a great option, delivering great results and a relatively low cost.

Technology has benefited many homeowners concerned about the security of their property, with a growing number of PC-based security systems, the values have become increasingly significant and even hurt in the pocket of those not so prepared to cover that extra expense.

The Arduino can help automate the home security, providing a compact solution (bringing together all in one device) to control PIR motion sensors, magnetic sensors, sirens, cameras, electric locks, signaling lights and more, and this with activation and deactivation controlled by safe codes handled directly on numeric keypads.

The type of residence, the number of rooms and the security profile you are looking for will define which sensors and modules to use, where you can employ PIR motion sensors to detect movements based on the variation of infrared light emitted by human body radiation, firing a siren if so, for example.

If you are using a large number of sensors, you may need to use an Arduino Mega, which has many more ports to connect than Arduino

Uno, which may provide greater possibilities, emphasizing that in both cases, the operation will be the same mode.

4 - Arduino Irrigation Project - Autonomous Greenhouse

Now the excuse is gone: "Puts, I forgot." Anyone who has a garden or greenhouse knows that they should water regularly. You may love flowers or have salads and vegetables in the greenhouse that you are eager to eat, but watering can be a challenge, especially if you are traveling or going out at night (this is because you should avoid watering during the day because water in conjunction with the scorching sun can burn the leaves).

So what now? Shouldn't I plant anything else? Calmly, the solution is Arduino home automation, where once again, it saves the day, allowing your garden to keep itself watered with the help of specially developed sensors.

Using specialized soil temperature and humidity sensors, Arduino can detect when plants need to be watered and trigger a solenoid valve or water pump, for example by meeting the need for plants housed in that particular location, because it will be able to Set when the land is dry and when it is wet (Real-time!), presented better results than those in which a person manages.

And what will I need? Some similar items already used so far and some specials, requiring 1 Arduino, 1 water pump or solenoid valve, 1 relay module, 1 Soil Moisture Sensor and Jumpers, and of course, that specific location type programming you want to automate, allowing you to stay alone. So now, this daily watering commitment

222

is no longer yours. For more details, go to the "Arduino Automatic Irrigation Project."

5 - Automatic Dog Feeder Design with Arduino

Pets are our partners in the house, whether cats or dogs, they need a lot of care especially, especially balanced and nutritious nutrition at the right time. But how do you control this if you work and stay away all day?

Excessive food is not good for the animal, the measure must be right and ruled with defined intervals between meals, i.e. leaving the bowl overflowing with food in the morning and forgetting for the rest of the day is not a good solution.

Nothing better than home automation with Arduino to break this deadlock and proportionate a healthy habit that will influence your pet's health. You are providing food at the right amount and at the right times.

I liked it, but how does it work? With a standalone feeder connected to the Internet, you can send commands to Arduino to feed your dog or cat at the right time or at scheduled times if using an RTC (Real Time Clock Module) connected to the microcontroller system.

Efficient and simple, the feeder is fixed in a place already stocked with ration, where a type of shovel stuck in an engine is responsible for dosing the amount of food, which motor is driven by Arduino as previously scheduled, to serve more or less, with a buzzer system to let the pet know it's time to eat.

For this automation, you will need 1 Arduino, 1 Relay Module, 1 Ethernet Shield (if you want to connect to the internet) or 1 RTC (if you want to work at pre-programmed times), 1 Motor, 1 Motor Driver, 1 Buzzer and Jumpers. Since here everything is possible, you can replace any component with another, being mere suggestions that may or may not be followed will depend on the will and possibilities of who will do the installation and programming.

Finally, these 5 project ideas are just a few possibilities for starting home automation with Arduino in your home and can be broadly extended due to a large number of sensors and electronics modules currently in existence. Check out every Arduino product line available on the website.

So which one are you going to do? Time to take Arduino off and put it to work. More than ever, the electronic revolution is approaching; perhaps one day, we may have a fully automated home, as intelligent as Iron Man's. While this day is not enough, let's kick-start, because this decade will be the machines!

www.ingramcontent.com/pod-product-compliance
Lightning Source LLC
Chambersburg PA
CBHW071112050326
40690CB00008B/1202